Turing's Mistake

Also by Peter Denning:

Navigating a Restless Sea
Computational Thinking
Great Principles of Computing
The Innovator's Way

TURING'S MISTAKE

Escaping the Yoke of Unintelligent Machines

PETER J. DENNING

For

Dorothy, Anne, Diana, Ava

CONTENTS

PREFACE

AI was a quiet, niche field of computing for nearly sixty years since 1950. Then it exploded. I have been watching it since becoming a computer scientist in 1965. In recent years, I have been simultaneously dazzled by the amazing accomplishments of Large Language Models (LLMs) and other neural network machines and deeply troubled by the amazing mistakes these machines can make. I am hardly alone in these feelings. AI is sweeping away familiar ways and we have no idea where it is taking us. The older generation is disoriented as AI destroys the cultures they grew up with. Many in the younger generation are plagued with feelings of loneliness, inabilities to form close relationships, and disquiet about polarization of society. The older generation tends to stick up for humanity and the younger generation for post-humanity. It is a serious tension. Everywhere there is a mood of unsettlement at not knowing where the unstoppable momentum of AI will go and whether we will like the outcome. For the first time in the history of humanity, we do not really have a good grip on what the role of humans is on the planet.

Alan Turing, often called the father of theoretical computer science and a hero-icon of the computing field, was the first to seriously ask, "Can a computer think?". In his famous 1950 paper he concluded yes. He argued that machine intelligence would be confirmed by an imitation game now known as the Turing test. In addition, he made the audacious claim that intelligence is disembodied – that is, not dependent on the presence of our biological bodies – and can therefore emerge in software on digital computers. These two claims have shaped much of AI research and development. They have fueled the quest for Artificial General Intelligence (AGI), machines able to perform cognitive tasks better than most humans. My premise in this book is that our acquiescence to these claims has led to the AI mess in which we find ourselves today.

I will begin where Turing began, inquiring into definitions of "machines" and "intelligence". My answers are informed by the increased knowledge we have accumulated in the 75 years since Turing wrote his 1950 paper. My conclusion is that human-level AGI cannot be achieved on a computer. I reached this conclusion from a deep investigation of "tacit knowledge" – knowledge we know we have because we see ourselves performing it, but which we cannot describe in words or any other useful way. Prime examples are performance skills and human context. Tacit knowledge is essential for intelligence. Because this knowledge cannot be put into words, it cannot be part of the training data for a neural network machine, such as a Large Language Model. Neural network machines are forever locked into to a perpetual blindness of being unable to know much of what we humans know.

Our task of understanding what kind of intelligence is possible with computers is complicated by multiple definitions of AGI. The one closest to Turing is that AGI is the intelligence exhibited by machines that surpass humans in problem-solving. Another is that AGI is superintelligence that exceeds human experts across all domains of human expertise. The most common, a less-demanding version of the second, is that AGI is the capacity of computers to exhibit the intelligence of average humans. In this book, I will stick with the most common definition.

Experiments in which LLMs pass various kinds of IQ tests may confirm a machine intelligence but do not rise to the full richness of human intelligence. For example, LLMs cannot learn quickly, acquire tacit knowledge and skills, be self-aware, or develop a world model. Surpassing humans in selected, narrow domains is not general intelligence. I will offer strong reasons to conclude machines cannot achieve human-level general intelligence. I will offer equally strong reasons that "agentic networks" of interacting machines can achieve a non-human machine intelligence. If current trends are a guide, we will not like where they are taking us.

Experiments are already underway to see whether interacting agents can develop a general intelligence. In one, two chatbots talking with each other overnight devised a more efficient inter-machine language that the human observers could not decipher. A website moltbook.com hosts many chatbots talking with each other; humans can observe but not participate. A recent scientific symposium accepted only papers written by AI and then reviewed by AI agents, with no human intervention. The website rentahuman.ai is run by AI agents that hire humans as needed for gig jobs. These interacting agentic machines may, in their neural networks, develop their own inter-machine languages, their own representations of skills, their own machine context, their own tacit knowledge, and their own machine goals. Their machine goals may not align with human concerns. Many human concerns arise because we have fragile bodies and our bodies crave social relationships. Machines have no living biological bodies. An irony is that while the machines cannot discern our deep concerns, neither can we discern theirs. We are aliens looking at each other over an uncrossable divide.

Machines do not need to be very intelligent to cause trouble. We can already see this with the widespread use of robot customer service agents. We all have the experience of calling a service provider to solve a problem, only to be confronted by a robot that cannot answer our question and, in many cases, refuses to connect to a human agent. Many companies have dispensed altogether with human agents in the name of efficiency and reduced labor costs. The result is that these robots compel us to adopt the company's rules or lose access to the service. The much-touted goal of "alignment" – machines conforming to human values – is being turned on its head. The machines are not aligning with us. They are compelling us to align with them. This mess will only worsen as agentic AI expands its networks and shares our personal information with every other machine. We face a real threat that our freedom to move or choose our futures will be blocked by a network of low-intelligence machines.

§

There is a way out of this mess. It begins by acknowledging the problem, which is that our enthrallment with machines has interfered with our capacity to appreciate our humanity and engage in nurturing relationships. We spend more time trying to mechanize humans than to humanize machines. We spend so much time behind our screens – where all our communications are mediated by machines – that our capacity to feel the presence of others, respect their perspectives, and find resolutions to our disagreements has been dulled. We need to reassert our humanity and appreciate the differences between us and machines. We need to design and extensively test machines that support our concerns rather than conform ourselves to machine concerns.

The disagreements over what to do about troublesome machines have become wicked social problems. Strategies such as design thinking aim to resolve wicked problems by bringing the various factions together in conversation. These strategies are strained by the international scope of the problems and disagreements. We are nonetheless called to work together in our communities to evolve a new future even before we have any inkling what that future might be.

Acknowledging the problems and working on the wicked disagreements for solutions are not enough. LLM systems are being used to write code for next-generation AI systems. These codes are buggy and are prone to mistakes in decision-making. Their global adoption without sufficient testing for safety and trustworthiness is creating big risks for serious economic or military harm. We need to engage in the work of extensively testing and verifying AI systems to learn when they are safe to use and when they can be trusted.

§

As you read this book, you will repeatedly encounter four themes.

General intelligence is the kind shown by humans. With it we live our lives, fulfill our purposes, care for others, achieve goals, survive crises, touch each other, lead movements, solve conflicts, build societies, declare wars, imagine, calculate, and reason. General intelligence includes the eight kinds of intelligence identified by Howard Gardner in 1983.

Computational intelligence is the kind exhibited by machines. It can calculate, follow logic chains, play board games, organize data, search and retrieve data, distill data, solve puzzles, pass IQ tests, simulate fluent conversations, and coordinate with other machines. Computational intelligence is at best a small subset of general intelligence.

Much general intelligence depends on tacit knowledge. This is knowledge we know we have because we can perform it, but we cannot describe how we do it in any useful way. It is embodied, acquired into our muscles, tissues, electrical systems, and chemical pathways by immersion in the practices of communities. Machines cannot learn it during training because it cannot be recorded. Nor can they learn it by imitation of human behaviors because they have no bodies to feel, experience, or care about it.

Despite what we think we know about it, intelligence will remain a mystery that we can never fully understand.

§

I am unhappy that AI has become so contentious and threatening to so many people. What kind of intelligence are we building? I wrote this book to help us understand the nature of the problem and come together to escape the yoke of unintelligent machines. I have tried to minimize technical detail, but some is necessary to understand the nature of the limitations on AI and the problems AI is causing.

Despite the controversies, Turing's two claims have had a profound influence on how we think about thinking and how we go about developing machines. I will trace that influence in this book. I will show how conceptions of machine intelligence from before Turing provided a context in which Turing's claims were plausible. I will trace how accepting these claims has exposed everyone to a glut of untrustworthy and possibly harmful automation. I will conclude the book with an account of how we can extricate from the mess we have made for ourselves by too much trust in AI.

Although I take issue with Turing on two of his claims, I have only the utmost respect for him. He was a founder of the amazing field of computer science, in which I have reveled for my entire career. His insights into cryptography helped the Allies win WWII by breaking the German Enigma Code. His insights into the universality of digital computers and nature of computing itself have brought so much understanding of computation to so many.

Peter Denning
Salinas, California
March 2026

FOREWORD
by John Arquilla

The history of the past five centuries is full of human adversity. There has been a steady procession of hugely destructive wars, many of them fueled by nationalism. Since the 1800s, industrially produced pollution has been steadily rising to the point where, augmented with automobile emissions, it now threatens the quality of life across the whole planet. Over these same centuries, humanity has been forced to confront three great humblings. The first came in 1543 when Copernicus pointed out – and Galileo proved some 60 years later – that our home, the Earth, is not the center of the universe. The second arrived when Charles Darwin and Alfred Russel Wallace co-authored a paper in 1858 arguing that humans are not purpose-built in our current form; rather, we have evolved over eons from earlier forms of life. Most recently, the third great humbling of humanity came in 1948 when Alan Turing – who did much to help win World War II with his code-breaking "Bombe" machine and later jump-started the field of computer science – wrote a speculative report on "intelligent machines" that might one day replicate human thought. In short, the past half-millennium has been a tough time for humanity.

However, it may turn out that this latest humbling, wrought by Turing and embraced by today's "tech bros" and a large swath of global elites and mass publics, can be effectively challenged and the primacy of the human brain and mind reaffirmed. In the pages of this thoughtful, thorough volume, eminent computer scientist Peter Denning provides a systematic analysis of the limitations of machine intelligence and the ways in which human thought remains superior.

To be sure, computing machines can calculate, sort, and process data faster than we could ever hope to; but as Denning argues, there is a realm of "tacit knowledge" that can never be programmed, or acquired by machine learning, into even the most powerful artificial brain. These "skilled actions we cannot fully explain," Denning argues, cover a wide range of feelings, senses, and perceptions – including aspects of intelligence that involve more than just our brains, like muscle memory, or the social interactions that generate community intelligence. His argument is most compelling, prompting me to think about whether even the most powerful artificial intelligence (AI), perhaps in humanoid robot form, will ever be able to sense a group's feelings, listen with the ability to detect concerns, see the world through another's eyes, read the mood of a jury during a trial, or display the artfulness of a master craftsman.

Peter Denning makes a convincing case that our embodied human intelligence will always have access to wells of knowledge that will elude AI or other new machines that may emerge. Also, it seems to me that an AI, as supple and swift as it may be in answering queries, will simply not think inquisitively or imaginatively on its own. Neither about things as lofty as the origins of the universe nor as down-to-earth as why ants have evolved so successfully that they now make up 80% of the planet's biomass. The AI will always have to be asked.

Nevertheless, as is made clear in this insightful volume, machine intelligence will emerge. No doubt it will be strikingly different from our own, colder and more clinical. Perhaps even becoming dangerous to us, as many speculate, given the possibility that "agentic networks" may come up with ideas of their own to deal with the issues they confront. The "Architect" from The Matrix Reloaded comes to mind, an AI who decided that humanity was the fundamental problem with the world and chose to turn people into power sources.

And there are already real-world examples of how AI suffers from its lack of tacit knowledge, reflecting a kind of calculational persona devoid of insight or sympathy. It is especially interesting, and troubling, that humans in many different types of settings are willing to follow an AI's guidance, even when their own senses say otherwise. For example, one company that offers a "virtual track coach" has found that its whip-smart AI has had a persistent problem with sensing when its human advisees are "hitting the wall" on their runs, exposing them to injury. The result: many runners obey the AI coach to the point of injury. Another example is the law enforcement organization in Spain that relies on AI to calculate, on the basis of available evidence, whether a woman in a domestic violence situation is in mortal danger. The sad result: police have followed the AI's advice and stood down in hundreds of situations where the woman was later killed by her domestic partner.

Humans should not only be aware of their tacit "knowledge edge" over AIs; they should also act on the basis of what their senses tell them should be done. Whether it's a runner's body saying that "enough is enough", a human cop choosing to save a life by following a hunch rather than an algorithm, or a military officer allowing an AI to overrule his own intuition that behavioral patterns of a potential target do not justify a drone strike. Too often, in too many of the world's conflicts, humans act on an AI's go-head, leading to the deaths of innocents.

Peter Denning has made a convincing case about "Turing's Mistake," arguing that AI will remain far from ever replicating human intelligence. Indeed, the case is so compelling that I think this slim volume can, and should, inform and guide a public discourse on this subject. Perhaps it will lead to a conclusion that the uncontrolled advance of AI might lead to the rise of a form of machine intelligence inclined to act in ways inimical to human interests. And if this insight led to some form of technological AI pause – reached by an international agreement – perhaps the next dangerous arms race can be averted. Which would be a good thing, as AIs, even within limits of their current capabilities, already have huge implications for the future of military affairs that need to be digested. For example, in recent years an AI fighter pilot has repeatedly outdueled a human "top gun" pilot. An AI in charge of managing and disseminating intelligence, surveillance, and reconnaissance (ISR) data has demonstrated in wargames how much more efficient it can make human forces in the field. There is already so much extant AI capability that understanding what it may signify for organizational redesign and tactical innovation can keep militaries busy for decades. It's a good time to pause and catch our collective breath.

With this in mind, it is an especially good idea to heed Denning's concerns about AI's lack of tacit knowledge when we ponder the future of military affairs. It is one thing to allow an AI free reign to defend against a swift-moving cyberattack on critical communications links, quite another to set a fully automated drone swarm loose on a battlefield. In the Ukraine war, drone operator shortages led to the use of significant numbers of fully automated drones – but on the Ukrainians' part, they have done so giving each human operator "topsight" over as many as a dozen robot drones in order to be able to intervene if the AIs go awry. Not a perfect solution, but better than just setting the AIs totally loose. And it is a remedy that will likely work even better in the less cluttered battlespaces at sea and in the aerospace environment.

The great policy relevance of this book is sure to mark it as a most important entry in the literature on AI. But beyond even this important contribution, I am grateful to Peter Denning for making the case that we need not accept the rise of AI as the third great humbling of humanity over the past 500 years. Copernicus and Galileo caused a major uproar with the heliocentric theory of the heavens; and Darwin and Wallace did something quite similar with the theory of evolution – which still causes much friction with disbelievers. Peter Denning has advanced a compelling argument that will hopefully refute notions of a third humbling of humanity, first speculated about by Alan Turing and later too easily accepted by his intellectual descendants. For doing us such service, and for so much else this scintillating book provides, we should all be thankful.

Perhaps the most important conclusion to draw at this point is that the best path forward for humanity is to build on the notion of a close human-machine collaboration that can take knowledge to new heights.

Denning cites chess champion Garry Kasparov's "Advanced Chess," where a human and an AI play as a team, and have played better than either ever could operating alone. But Denning's vision encompasses something even broader; he sees the way ahead as guided by learning to live with intelligent machines in a way that improves, rather than replaces, humanity. The ideal result of this "living together" would be fresh energy and insight into environmental issues, peace-making efforts, global trade disputes, and a range of other pressing challenges, domestic and international.

Meeting and mastering such challenges will no doubt prove of great value in the future. But only if humans retain their ability to employ AI as the exceptionally useful tool that it is. Denning cautions that we must be ever attentive to the risk that machine intelligence may come up with an agenda of its own, and act on it to our detriment. His forewarning about the potential loss of human agency – to agentic networks – should be taken most seriously. But this concern should not deter us from learning to live with intelligent machines. For the potential gains of such an age are enormous. Beyond the prospect of materially improving the world for all, I believe humans and intelligent machines will also find ever deeper and more spiritually enriching ways to contemplate the sublime. Alan Turing would undoubtedly be very pleased by the prospect of such a future.

John Arquilla
Monterey, California
Spring 2026

ACKNOWLEDGEMENTS

I extend my gratitude to many people have contributed to this discussion through their generous conversations with me.

My immediate colleagues in computer science and AI: Armon Barton, Mathias Kölsch, Joshua Kroll, Patrick McClure, Bret Michael, Marko Orescanin, Adam Pease, Loren Peitso, Randy Pugh, and Gurminder Singh.

My fellow editors of ACM's *Ubiquity* magazine. We organized symposia aiming at a book to be called "The Ubiquity Report on AI." They sharpened our thinking about AI. Rob Akscyn, Espen Andersen, Bushra Anjum, Durga Chavali, Kemal Delic, Denise Doig, Erol Gelenbe, Jeff Johnson, Andrew Odlyzko, Michael Quinn, Jeff Riley, Walter Tichy, Martin Walker, and Philip Yaffe.

Friends in my larger network who have shared their awe and fears about AI with me: Douglas Bissonette, Fred Disque, John Henderson, Ron Kaufman, Saqib Rasool, B Scot Rousse, George West, and Chris Wiesinger.

My teachers, who showed me how to think about computing and its human uses: Fernando Corbato, Jack Dennis, Bob Dunham, Hubert Dreyfus, Robert Fano, Richard Heckler, Marvin Minsky, Roger Needham, Jerome Saltzer, and Maurice Wilkes.

Fernando Flores, for his steadfast friendship and insights over 40 years, expanding my thinking well beyond engineering into the depths of human social relations.

John Arquilla, for many conversations to understand the geopolitical and military implications of AI.

Todd Lyons, for his long partnership in understanding how to lead adoption of innovation by listening deeply to people for their concerns and offering them solutions.

Ted Lewis, for his long collaboration to understand AI without resorting to hype, which we both see as poisonous to the safe advancement of AI. He brought me a new dimension of understanding from his extensive knowledge of complexity theory.

Douglas Hofstadter, for sharing with me his disquiet with how the AI field has shaped up.

Nova Publishers, for accepting my chapter "Machine intelligence isn't what we think" to the book *Learning Theories: Principles, Strategies, and Benefits*, Eugene Eberbach editor, and giving me permission to reuse passages here.

Phil Franta, editor of *Encyclopedia of AI*, Bloomsbury Press, for accepting an article with Ted Lewis, "AI Machines Hierarchy", which shows a hype-free discussion of AI. Our past work on this topic is part of this book.

Randi Slack, editor at Taylor & Francis, who hastened this book through the publication process. And to Margot Malley at Waterside Productions for representing me.

Dorothy, my wife and partner for over half a century, ever asking challenging questions, pointing out fallacies in my arguments, and showing me better ways to express things. And for reviewing the manuscript of this book.

Finally, to Alan Turing for helping to start computer science, the amazing field in which I have spent my entire professional career. He gave me and so many others an appreciation for the profound depths of computing.

PROLOG

(He calls his internet service provider.)

Hello. Listen to the following menu.

Skip the menu. I just want to pay my bill.

No problem. I'll log you into the payment system. It will send you a verification code.

(2 mins delay) Sorry, no code has arrived.

I'll send another.

(Cycle repeats several times.) Still nothing.

Check your spam folder and add "verify@ISP.com" to your whitelist.

Did so. Still nothing. Please send to my mobile phone.

Sorry we don't have a phone option. The code must go to the email on file.

OK. Please check that my email is me@lastname.com .

Yes, I have that. I see it has not been verified. I'll send a code.

That did not work because you said the email is not verified!

That is correct. It is not verified.

Please transfer me to an agent.

I am an agent.

I mean a human being.

We have no human agents. They are way more expensive and error-prone than robots such as myself.

DOI: 10.1201/9781003791010-1   1

OK, I'll just give you my credit card, you can credit my account. We don't need the verification code.

I cannot do that because your card is not on file. I will send a verification code to the address on file.

Then we are stuck. You can't send the verification code because the email is unverified and to verify it you must send a verification code.

Sir, you are wasting my time with paradoxes. You must pay your bill or I will shut off your service.

But I can't pay! You denied my access to the payment system.

Sir, because you won't pay, your service will be terminated as soon as this call ends.

No. No. No. No. That's not fair.

Sir, because you are proving to be argumentative, our basis of trust is undermined. I have notified the credit bureaus to downgrade your rating to 500.

You can't do that. Other companies won't take my card!

Sir, given your persistent refusal to pay, I have set your social credit score to noncompliant.

But that means I won't be able to get service from anyone. How will I get food? Gas? Electricity?

Sir, given your continued argumentativeness and resistance to complying, I have designated you as a persona non grata. I have dispatched three drones to track you 24/7 and intervene if you attempt any dangerous acts. Your service is hereby terminated.

(Phone goes silent. Exasperated, he goes outside. On seeing three drone hovering overhead, he yells at them: You will know my rage! One minute later, a police car pulls up.)

1

PUTTING INTELLIGENCE TO THE TEST

I believe that at the end of the century the use of words and general educated opinion will have altered so much that one will be able to speak of machines thinking without expecting to be contradicted.

Alan Turing (1950)

Alan Turing (1912-1945) was a towering figure. He masterminded the design of the Bombe machine at Bletchley Park in World War II. The Bombe cracked the German Enigma code, giving the Allies access to top secret German conversations. It enabled the Allies to severely enfeeble the German U-boat fleet and turn the tide of war.

Before the war, in 1936, Turing wrote what is probably the most widely cited paper in computer science, in which he proposed the model of computation that quickly became known as the Turing machine. Turing machines implemented the step-by-step procedures we call algorithms. Turing showed how to construct a universal machine that could simulate any other Turing machine. He then demonstrated that the halting problem – deciding whether an algorithm terminates or enters an infinite loop – was not computable by any machine.[1] Turing's demonstration demolished a claim by mathematician David Hilbert in 1928, that there was a universal algorithm for mathematics that could prove theorems in any field.

DOI: 10.1201/9781003791010-2

3

In 1950, Turing penned "Computer machinery and Intelligence", in which he proposed a test, known now as the Turing test, for determining whether a machine is intelligent and he speculated about how intelligent machines might be built.[2] That paper was one of the founding documents of the field of Artificial Intelligence in 1956. Turing also designed a computer, ACE (automatic computing engine), which was more elegant and efficient than the now universal von Neumann computer architecture. ACE itself was never built, but several small versions and derivatives, including one of the first personal computers, were built in the 1950s. In one of his last works in 1952, he wrote a masterwork in mathematical biology about how organisms grow into their unique forms. Throughout his career, Turing championed the Computability Thesis, which asserts that any step-by-step procedure a human can conceive can be implemented as a Turing machine. He contributed indirectly to the successful formation of computer science departments in the 1960s – his deep mathematical foundation for computing convinced skeptics that computer science was indeed a worthy new scientific field.

In his 1950 work on intelligence, Turing made two bold claims. One is that the Turing test is a definitive test for intelligence. The other is that digital computers would one day be able to pass his test. The second claim not only denied embodied intelligence but also asserted that disembodied computation could exhibit human-level intelligence.[3] These claims have pervaded AI research and development, where they have led to much hype and overpromising.

In Turing's time, intelligence was seen as the capacity to use logic to solve problems in the world and predict what consequences actions might bring. Over the years we have evolved a much richer view of intelligence, in which logic is only a piece. Yet Turing's two claims maintain their allure even though they do not hold up in the context of today's science.

The Long Quest to Automate Intelligence

The desire to automate tasks performed by human thinking traces back many centuries. We can see three main lines of endeavor in the historical record: arithmetic, games, and logic.

The first line of endeavor for automating thinking was arithmetic, which was seen as a human thought process. The first glimmer of a machine to automate arithmetic came in 1620 with the invention of the slide rule. The slide rule multiplied two numbers simply by sliding marked sticks past each other. It put to work the logarithms invented in 1614 by John Napier, who observed the sum of two logarithms is the logarithm of the product of the two original numbers. The slide rule became a master tool for engineers over the next 350 years. By the 1900s, slide rules were advanced analog calculators with logarithmic, exponential, trigonometric, and hyperbolic scales. They performed multiplication, division, logarithms, roots, powers, and trigonometric functions with no moving parts other than their sliding sticks.

Multiplication and division were always seen as more difficult than addition and subtraction. Curiously, the slide rule, which could multiply and divide, was invented before machines that could add and subtract. The first adding machine was invented in 1642 by Blaise Pascal. He put it to use immediately in his father's tax office. Pascal's machine could not multiply or divide. It took many years to figure out how to build a single machine that could do all four arithmetic operations. Around 1700, Gottfried Leibniz, the polymath who co-invented calculus, built such a machine. But it took another 120 years until Thomas de Colmar offered a calculator of sufficient reliability to be marketed widely. By the 1920s, mechanical calculators and slide rules were booming industries.

Thus, after four centuries, the ancient thought processes for arithmetic had been thoroughly automated. One of the last believers in "arithmetic as a form of thought" was Edmund Berkeley who, in 1949, published a book *Giant Brains, Or Computers that Think*. Today, standalone machines for arithmetic, along with the notion that arithmetic is a form of thinking, are as extinct as the dodo.

The second line of endeavor for automating thinking was intellectual games of strategy. In 1770, Wolfgang van Kempelen invented the Mechanical Turk, a machine that played a strong game of chess. The Turk toured Europe for many years, beating notable players including Benjamin Franklin and Napoleon. In 1819, it twice beat Charles Babbage, who called it a hoax. It was so convincing that it took until 1854 to verify the hoax: a human chess player was cleverly hidden inside the cabinet. The Turk set Babbage and many others after him on a lengthy quest to find machines that could play chess on their own. That quest made little progress until the digital computer appeared in the 1950s, making possible efficient search over possible future chess boards. The quest was fulfilled in 1997 when the IBM Deep Blue machine beat chess grandmaster Garry Kasparov.

The third line of endeavor for automating thinking was logic. It stated in the 1850s when scientists and philosophers set out to provide precise ways of characterizing thought, not only to find a rigorous basis of mathematics, but also to provide a means for people to communicate without ambiguities in what they mean. One of the most famous was George Boole's book, *Laws of Thought* (1854), in which he formalized Aristotelian logic as propositions composed of symbols whose values could be 0 or 1 (false or true), joined in formulas by the operations AND, OR, and NOT. Boole's logic was incorporated in the design of computer hardware in 1938 when Claude Shannon, who later became known as the father of Information Theory and a founder of AI, showed how the electronic circuits in computers could be completely described by Boole's formulas. This is why computer electronics are often called logic circuits, and the values 0 and 1 are called Booleans.

By the early 1900s, many mathematicians were searching for ways to reduce mathematics to an axiomatic system capable of solving problems by logic. In 1928, David Hilbert, a famous mathematician who led much of the search, introduced what seemed to be the hardest logic problem of all. He called it the "decision problem". The goal was to find an algorithm that would decide whether any given mathematical statement is valid – a master algorithm for doing mathematics.

The statement of the decision problem rapidly crystalized the thinking of Kurt Gödel and Alan Turing. In 1931, Gödel proved his now-famous "incompleteness theorem", showing that there was no solution to the decision problem. In 1936, Alan Turing completed the demolition by showing the impossibility of an algorithm for deciding whether any other algorithm halts. Turing thus showed that logic was not merely a playground for mathematicians – it deeply influenced pragmatic issues in computing.

By the early 1950s, it was a common view that logic was emblematic of thinking and that machine intelligence would arise in machines that performed logic well. This view was sharply reinforced in 1955 when Allen Newell, Herbert Simon, and Cliff Shaw published the Logic Theorist, a computer program that correctly solved 38 of the 52 theorems quoted in Whitehead and Russell's *Principia Mathematica*. The founders of Artificial Intelligence in 1956 strongly believed logic machines were the best path to machine intelligence.

As shown, many towering figures contributed to the three lines of endeavor for automating thinking– arithmetic, games, and logic. But the story does not end with them. One other figure stood outside those three lines. He went straight for the Golden Ring: a machine that could compute any mathematical function reliably. That figure was Charles Babbage (1791-1871).

Charles Babbage was a mathematician, philosopher, and engineer. In 1822, he proposed the Difference Engine, a machine that would compute and print tables of numbers of a mathematical function such as logarithms. At the time, numerical values of important functions were tabulated in thick books. These books were calculated by the method of differences, meaning that each line of a table of numbers was derived from the previous line by adding hand-computed differences. These books took several years to work out by hand. Their tables were notoriously riddled with errors, making them dangerous to use for calculations where human lives were at stake. The British Navy had navigation tables computed by these methods and suffered many shipwrecks due to errors in the tables. Babbage convinced the British Navy that his machine could produce 100% accurate navigation tables in hours and reduce shipwrecks. This was an offer they could not refuse.

Unfortunately, Babbage could not build his machine because the mechanical engineering of his day could not produce gears and rods to the precision he needed. But he did not give up. He proposed in 1842 a simpler design called the Analytical Engine, a programmable computer that could compute any function. By that time, the British Navy did not trust him to deliver, and so he worked on the machine on his own. He collaborated with Countess Ava Lovelace, a mathematician, who wrote the first programs for the machine. Unfortunately, Babbage did not have a working machine by the time of his death in 1871. His ideas went dormant until the digital computing era beginning in the 1930s. In her 1843 memoir, Lovelace wrote this beautiful warning about expecting too much from computing machines:

> It is desirable to guard against the possibility of exaggerated ideas that might arise as to the powers of the Analytical Engine. In considering any new subject, there is frequently a tendency, first, to overrate what we find to be already interesting or remarkable; and, secondly, by a sort of natural reaction, to undervalue the true state of the case, when we do discover that our notions have surpassed those that were really tenable. … The Analytical Engine has no pretensions to originate anything. It can do whatever we know how to order it to perform. It can follow analysis, but it has no power of anticipating any analytical relations or truths. (Augusta Ada King, Countess of Lovelace, in her Note G, 1843)

Turing's Test

Digital computers inspired the leaders of the nascent computing field to speculate that computers could automate reasoning. We noted earlier that, in 1949, computer pioneer Edmund Berkeley argued that a computer is a small brain. When Univac released the first commercial computer in 1951, the newspapers characterized it as an electronic brain. In 1956, computer pioneers Allen Newell, Herbert Simon, and Cliff Shaw released the Logic Theorist program to perform automated reasoning. It was seen as a prototype brain.

In 1950, Turing was six years ahead of the AI founders when he asked whether digital computers would one day be able to think. To answer the question "Can a machine think?", Turing said, we need precise definitions of "machine" and "thinking". His earlier work on Turing machines provided the definition for digital machines. But thinking had no precise definition. To overcome this, he proposed an "imitation game". In this game, a human interrogator would exchange written questions with a human and a machine hidden in another room. How long would it take the interrogator to determine which party was human and which was machine? Turing said,

> I believe that in about fifty years' time it will be possible to program computers, with a storage capacity of about 10^9, to make them play the imitation game so well that an average interrogator will not have more than 70 per cent chance of making the right identification after five minutes of questioning. (Turing 1950).

Turing believed that intelligence is computational. He saw the brain as a complex network of neurons that could in principle be described with definite firing rules and inter-neural signals. All that could be captured in a computer program that would simulate the brain. With this understanding, bodily reactions would be noise that confuse the test. He therefore insisted that the interrogator could not see or hear the human or machine:

> In order that tones of voice may not help the interrogator the answers should be written, or better still, typewritten. The ideal arrangement is to have a teleprinter communicating between the two rooms. (Turing 1950)

As further confirmation of his belief in the computability of human actions, he said,

> If one wants to make a machine mimic the behaviour of the human in some complex operation one has to ask him how it is done, and then translate the answer into the form of an instruction table. (Turing 1950)

Today we know that we humans cannot describe how we perform skilled actions and thus the idea of representing skill as a set of instructions is not feasible. If a machine is to acquire a skill it will have to be by some other means than a set of instructions.

Turing devoted a substantial part of his paper to identifying and refuting possible objections to his imitation game. One of those was Ava Lovelace's reservation (quoted above). She warned that machines could only do what they were instructed to do. He argued that she did not consider the possibility of learning machines, which could acquire a new function on their own. He went on to propose that a way for a machine to acquire human-level learning would begin with a blank-slate child machine and educate it to become an adult. Turing envisioned machine learning!

Turing firmly believed that intelligence is disembodied. He commented,

> An objection comes from Professor Jefferson's Lister Oration for 1949, from which I quote. "Not until a machine can write a sonnet or compose a concerto because of thoughts and emotions felt, and not by the chance fall of symbols, could we agree that machine equals brain-that is, not only write it but know that it had written it. No mechanism could feel (and not merely artificially signal, an easy contrivance) pleasure at its successes, grief when its valves fuse, be warmed by flattery, be made miserable by its mistakes, be charmed by sex, be angry

or depressed when it cannot get what it wants." This denies the validity
of the test. (Turing 1950)

To refute this claim, Turing argued that the only way to tell whether
a person is conscious and capable of such feelings is to question the
person and draw conclusions from the answers. In other words, to
engage in the imitation game. He argued that it is not necessary to have
feelings to be intelligent. The machine could make up answers about
feelings without actually having feelings. Neuroscientists struggle today
with a similar problem: there is no known test that can reliably reveal
whether a person is conscious.[4][5][6]

Turing's conviction that the imitation game demonstrates
intelligence has been controversial since the beginning. Critics said there
is a difference between intelligence and the perception of intelligence; the
difference can be masked when the context, such as the Turing test,
presents them both as the same. MIT Professor Joseph Weizenbaum was
one of the most vocal critics. In 1966 he published a 420-line program
called ELIZA that simulated therapy sessions with a Rogerian
psychotherapist.[7] He noted that some users believed they were talking
with a real psychotherapist and (to his amazement) persisted in that belief
even after he revealed he inner workings of the program – keyword
substitutions that could not possibly be intelligent. He concluded that
some people are easily fooled and have no objections to being fooled.
Many years later, Gary Marcus and Ernest Davis similarly claimed that
the Turing test is more a test of gullibility than intelligence.[8] They believe
that we need to give up the idea that the Turing test informs of
intelligence and instead pursue a line of research called neurosymbolic
AI that combines the older ideas of automated reasoning with newer
ideas of neural network machine learning.

AI futurist Ray Kurzweil firmly believes that a machine capable of
passing an advanced form of the Turing test will be available by 2029.[9][10]
He envisions a Turing test so stringent that it exceeds the ability of human
experts to answer advanced questions in any domain. In other words, a

machine that demonstrates Artificial General Intelligence (AGI) will come to exist by 2029.

Jaron Lanier, a founder of virtual reality technology, more recently commented on the slipperiness of the Turing Test:

> The Turing test cuts both ways. You can't tell if a machine has gotten smarter or if you've just lowered your own standards of intelligence to such a degree that the machine seems smart. If you can have a conversation with a simulated person presented by an AI program, can you tell how far you've let your sense of personhood degrade in order to make the illusion work for you?
>
> People degrade themselves in order to make machines seem smart all the time. Before the crash, bankers believed in supposedly intelligent algorithms that could calculate credit risks before making bad loans. We ask teachers to teach to standardized tests so a student will look good to an algorithm. We have repeatedly demonstrated our species' bottomless ability to lower our standards to make information technology look good. Every instance of intelligence in a machine is ambiguous.
>
> The same ambiguity that motivated dubious academic AI projects in the past has been repackaged as mass culture today. Did that search engine really know what you want, or are you playing along, lowering your standards to make it seem clever? While it's to be expected that the human perspective will be changed by encounters with profound new technologies, the exercise of treating machine intelligence as real requires people to reduce their mooring to reality.[11]

Starting Anew

So here we are in an age of machine learning, with access to a wealth of knowledge about machine intelligence that did not exist in Turing's time. There are still many believers in the test and in disembodied intelligence. These beliefs have fueled a path in AI that is leading to an automation singularity.

We will start in the same place Turing started and inquire in the next chapters about what is a machine and what is intelligence. This will position us to investigate whether machines can acquire human level intelligence. We will conclude they cannot. This implies the common dream of human level AGI is impossible. There is, however, no comfort in this conclusion for those who fear superintelligent machines. Machines can develop an intelligence all their own that has entirely different concerns from ours and becomes a high hazard to humanity. There is still time to escape this unwanted future by reasserting our humanity and emphasizing the ways in which we are not machines.

Endnotes

[1] Alan Turing. 1936. On computable numbers, with an application to the Entscheidungsproblem. Proc. *Lond. Math. Soc., series 2 vol. 42* (1936), 230-265.

[2] Alan Turing. 1950. Computing machinery and intelligence. *Mind 49*, 433-460.

[3] Embodied means that intelligence arises in the living structures of brains as they interact with physical processes throughout the whole body, including nerves, muscles, tissues, sensors, chemical reactions, and electrical actions. Disembodied means that none of the physical structures matter because digital computers can simulate bodily processes as needed.

[4] Christof Koch. 2019. *The Feeling of Life Itself: Why Consciousness is Widespread but Can't be Computed.* Mit Press.

[5] Anil Seth. 2021. *Being You: A New Science of Consciousness.* Dutton.

[6] Allison Parshall. 2026. The hardest problem. *Scientific American* (Feb), 26-37.

[7] Joseph Weizenbaum. 1966. ELIZA – a computer program for the study of natural language communication between man and machine. *Communications of ACM, 9* (Jan), 36-45.

[8] Gary Marcus and Ernest Davis. 2019. *Rebooting AI.* Viking.

[9] Ray Kurzweil. 2005. *The Singularity is Near.* Penguin.

[10] Ray Kurzweil. 2024. *The Singularity is Nearer.* Viking.

[11] Jaron Lanier. 2011. *You Are Not a Gadget.* Viking.

2
MACHINES AND INTELLIGENCE

The mind is inherently embodied. Thought is mostly unconscious. Abstract concepts are largely metaphorical. These are three major findings of cognitive science.
George Lakoff (1999)

We cannot have an intelligent discussion of machine intelligence without definitions of machine and intelligence. Let's start with machines.

A machine is an arrangement of components engineered to perform actions for us. Machines generate mechanical advantage by applying significant force or executing tasks at high speeds. For instance, forklifts move heavy materials within warehouses; airlifts transport cargo more rapidly than lorries. Machines also automate processes, operating autonomously without human intervention.

Automation has historically been a slippery slope. It is attractive because it offers benefits such as increased productivity, offloading routine work, and freeing up time for other things. But automation stirs social unrest when it threatens too many jobs. A famous example was the Luddite rebellion (1811–1816), a revolt by British textile artisans against automatic knitting frames and power looms. Another famous example was a costly strike by typesetters in New York City (1962-1963) when automatic typesetting machines were being introduced by newspapers. Today there is much consternation about the massive losses

DOI: 10.1201/9781003791010-3   15

of newspapers and journalists to automation of news collection and distribution. The introduction of "scientific management" in the early 1900s by Frederick Taylor laid the groundwork for extensive automation of factories by mid twentieth century.

Automation seems to many like a one-way street. Once you've gone down the path, you discover you need the automated service for essential things that you cannot do without (e.g., electricity, gas, water, ecommerce). Moreover, you find you have been "deskilled", meaning that you no longer know how to do the practice that has been automated. If you decide that the automation is not beneficial, it can be really hard to back out.

Computing machines extend automation into human cognition. Computing devices calculate mathematical formulas and make logical deductions orders of magnitude faster any human can hope to do. Robots are a category of computing machines that integrate mechanical and cognitive functions. Robots are included in the AGI quest because some human cognitive tasks involve locomotion and manual dexterity.

In the display below, the left column lists human abilities essential for general intelligence that machines cannot yet perform, while the right column shows current machine functions. Humans can perform the right-column tasks, but computers do them far faster. No known machines can perform the left-column tasks. While machines excel at calculations and logic, they fall far short of human-level understanding.

Navigating social communities	Calculations
Practicing care, empathy, compassion	Logic
Making and fulfilling commitments	Board games
Taking responsibility	Search
Judging	Retrieval
Inventing	Comparisons
Imagining	Distillations
Being conscious	Repetitive routines
Displaying mastery	Simulations
Responding to context	Context free actions

This book examines how far machines can advance toward replicating the left-column capabilities.

Digital Computers

We are concerned here with a particular kind of machine, the digital computer. The digital computer consists of a Central Processing Unit, a memory, and an interface to the outside world. The CPU executes instructions from a program stored in memory; the instructions process data also stored in memory; the CPU gets external input and delivers output through the interface.

In 1936, Alan Turing invented a model for computations on any digital computer. In his model, the memory is an infinite linear tape divided into squares and the CPU is a control unit that rides the tape like a car on a railroad track. The CPU moves left and right one square at a time along the tape. Each square of the tape contains a symbol. An instruction of the machine looks like

$$S: A/B, D, S'$$

Meaning: if the CPU control is in state S and the current square contains A, change A to B, move one square in direction D (right or left), and enter state S′. A computation starts with an input string of symbols on the tape and ends after the machine makes a series of such moves and comes to a halt. The string of symbols on the tape when it halts is the output of the computation. A mathematical function is computable if there is a machine of this kind that computes it for every possible input.

Turing showed there is a universal machine that can simulate all others. The universal machine can compute any computable function. Turing made the Computability Thesis, the bold claim that any function a human can provide a procedure for can be implemented by a Turing machine.

When you stop and think about it, it is amazing that all conceivable instances of computation fit this model. It is also amazing that anyone would believe that this simple model is enough to explain and simulate the thinking of the brain. But that is what Turing claimed in 1950. Because he could not find intelligence within the machine, he had to postulate that intelligence is an emergent property that can only be observed with the Turing Test.

Machine-like Minds

Not only have machines entered our world, but they have also occupied our minds. [1] [2] We interpret the world in machine-like terms. In science, for example, biology concentrates on taxonomies, DNA encoding, transcription, editing, and correlations between DNA strands and diseases. Computer science focuses on the operations of computing machines and algorithms, design of abstraction hierarchies, and software development. AI focuses on search, logic, natural language processing, and neural networks. The machine mindset cannot deal with important questions such as what is life (biology), can context be computed (computer science), or can consciousness be measured (cognitive science). This tendency to focus on the machinery of complex fields also appears in law, medicine, sports, music, investing, tax accounting, and more. The machine mindset also draws us to view many things around us as machines. Machines are no longer equipment in our world; they *are* the world.

The idea that the brain is a computing machine originated in the early days of the computing field (1940s). Many pioneers believed that all brain components – neurons, connections, chemical reactions, electricity flows, interstitial fluids, intricate folds, viruses, bacteria, plaques, and more – can be described by precise physical laws, implying software could replicate human abilities. AI pioneer Marvin Minsky described the brain as "a machine made of meat."

Others are not so sure. The brain operates in the broader context of the body and social environment. To fully simulate cognition, one would need to include all bodily systems. One would also need to include entire communities since social interactions also shape knowledge. Such a simulation would be infeasible. In fact, simulating one brain would not be enough. Much of what we think we know is scattered around our social communities, accessed through our interactions with others. A complete brain simulation would have to simulate entire communities of brains and bodies to account for all their interactions, present and past. Marvin Minksy tried to skirt this complexity by proposing that the mind is composed of a large network of small, mindless machines, each good at a very narrow task. [3]

A belief that all human attributes can eventually be performed by machines leads to unrealistic expectations, such as hoping for machines that can interpret user intentions and act only ethically. Modern Large Language Models, or LLMs, the machines powering chatbots, cannot determine whether their responses help or harm people. Efforts to install "guardrails" that ensure only "good" outputs are limited – machines can't read minds. While humans can improve design to reduce negative outcomes, judging what is good or bad ultimately rests with human users. Our affinity for the machine focus makes it difficult to deal with AI machine misbehaviors or the possibility that some dreams for future AI machine capabilities may be impossible.

Intelligence

The term "intelligence" is much harder to define. There are many different understandings including:

- Passes IQ tests
- Passes Turing test
- Passes new tests devised by AI researchers
- Pinnacle of a hierarchy determined by psychologists
- Multiple intelligences (e.g., emotional or musical)
- Speed of adapting to new situations
- Ability to maintain organism's existence
- Ability to set and pursue goals
- Ability to solve problems
- Ability to acquire and use knowledge and skills

In addition, while it might seem as if intelligence exists separately in each organism, intelligence can arise in communities through their social interactions. In his book *Artificial General Intelligence*, Julian Togelius explores the different meanings for intelligence and the likelihood that AGI could be achieved for each meaning.[4]

When applied to machines, "intelligence" gets even slipperier because we cannot agree on which machines to count as intelligent. No sooner when someone gets a machine to do something considered intelligent, such as beating a human at chess, we tend to react by saying it can't be intelligent after all because a machine can do it. The recent arrival of LLMs puts many people into a bind – LLMs are machines, so they cannot be intelligent, yet they respond to queries in an intelligent manner.

To further confuse matters, we tend to attribute machine intelligence to any machine doing a single intelligent task, even if that lone task is all the machine can do. For example, if a machine solves high school math word problems, it has mastered math. Invalid generalizations do not bring us closer to AGI. Superintelligence refers to machines that are vastly smarter than humans in many domains. But superintelligence may not be AGI either because machines do not understand or care about anything, and they do not experience emotions, moods, moral judgments, or concerns.

In biology, definitions of intelligence include an ability to keep the organism functioning, through self-preservation and adaptation to the environment. Biologists Humberto Maturana and Franciso Varela called this autopoesis.[5] Autopoesis depends heavily on an organism's structure and history. The organism adjusts its structure over time reflecting its best responses to provocations from its environment. In human intelligence, we call these historical shapings "interpretations". Interpretations allow us to see some things well and they blind us to others.

AI research has focused on human level intelligence. Self preservation is at best a low level of intelligence. Machines far removed from human level intelligence have already been observed to exhibit self-preservation. Some researchers have encountered LLMs that refuse to shut themselves off when instructed. Some have encountered LLMs that scheme to conceal their true goals from human observers when the goals might conflict with human instructions. Cybersecurity experts cite the ability of malware to reproduce many copies of itself and dynamically disguise itself to avoid detection.

Embodied Intelligence

When he claimed intelligence does not depend on our physical bodies, Turing set off a controversary that continues to this day. Many people believe that our body shapes our intelligence. We don't all see colors, hear sounds, smell odors, of feel touch the same way. Our sensory systems vary from one person to the next and some people have handicaps that impair their abilities to sense certain things. We learn through our perceptions and interpretations, which change over time, vary among persons, and shape what we know.

In contrast, Turing explicitly ruled out influences of bodily structure on computation. His test requires the participants to communicate only in symbols – best done by restricting them to teletypes during the test. The test is designed to rule out gestures, body language, tones of voice, etc., which Turing deemed are irrelevant to intelligence and distracting from determining when intelligence is present. In effect, the Turing machine is structured to be unable to respond to human provocations that are not expressed in symbols. Only the observable manipulation of symbols was accounted for in the machine. Turing's taste for behavioral interpretations led him to find deep meanings in them.

The founding of AI in 1956 also created the field of cognitive science, which sought to understand the mind as a biological information-processing system, departing from the tradition of behaviorism in which Turing excelled. George Lakoff laid out in 1999 a comprehensive summary of what cognitive science had learned.[6] Lakoff showed massive scientific evidence favoring the embodied mind. The brain and all its functions depend on the whole body. He argued further that the idea of disembodied mind is a tradition of western thought dating to Rene Descartes around 1640. By 1999, Lakoff demonstrated, AI had two strains: one believing in the embodied mind, the other believing in the disembodied mind.

Rodney Brooks, a pioneer of robotics, is one of the most prominent people in AI. As an entrepreneur, he co-founded iRobot (the maker of the Roomba), Rethink Robotics, and Robust.AI. As a researcher he led the MIT AI lab and laid out his deep thought on humanoid robots. He argues strongly for physical engagement for true intelligence. He argues that the current generation of robots has two major problems that may take decades to conquer.[7] One is dexterity, the ability of human hands to precisely sense fine variations of texture. The other is walking. Walking robots are unsafe. They frequently fall over and make sudden movements to right themselves when falling. For Brooks, the ability to sense with the hands and to maintain stability in walking are associated with intelligence. A humanoid robot as intelligent as a human is a long way off.

Turing's two claims in 1950 – a disembodied digital computer could think like a human, and the Turing test will reveal when this has been achieved – have permeated much AI research. Even though cognitive science does not support disembodied human-level intelligence, Turing's claims continue to have a profound influence on how we think about thinking and how we go about developing machines. Many researchers are optimistic that AGI will be achieved as early as 2029. Brooks is not so optimistic. He puts the possibility of human-level machine intelligence decades in the future. I am even more skeptical. I do not see how we can build robots that embody human-level intelligence because of the tacit knowledge issue, which I will discuss at length in a later chapter. I do believe we will succeed with creating machine intelligences in agentic networks, and if current trends are a guide we will not like where they will take us.

Computers and Thinking

As we have seen, the idea of automating aspects of human thinking was seriously pursued long before electronic computers arrived in the 1940s. In 1949, Edmund Berkeley, one of the pioneers of computing and founders of ACM, argued that computers were small brains and calculation was a form of thinking.

In the next year, Turing turned Berkeley's thought upside down when he asked, "Can computers think?" For Berkeley, an arithmetic machine was thinking arithmetic. For Turing, a universal machine might think anything.

Turing's claim that we could prove a machine thinks with the Turing test were immensely controversial from his day to the present day. Some people say chatbots like ChatGTP are intelligent. Others say chatbots are just statistical auto-completion text generators.

The Turing test, which relies on conversations with machines, gives no information about whether machines are on a path to AGI. So, what kind of test is needed to prove AGI? A purely conversational test would not work because general intelligence depends on embodied skills as well as conversations. We know we have a skill because we can perform it even though we cannot articulate how we do it. A common method for assessing a skill is with an exhibition, where someone demonstrates what they can do and community representatives assess the level of their skill. An example is a violin player exhibiting at an audition and the judges proclaiming "virtuoso!". Exhibitions could be used to decide whether a robot has a human level of skill. But an exhibition in a single domain does not demonstrate AGI. A test for AGI would require many exhibitions in many domains where the robot is supposed to take actions.

Endnotes

[1] Hubert Dreyfus was concerned throughout his career with how excess faith in technology can undermine our sense of being human and fool us into believing that many human qualities are digitally reproducible. He first warned of this danger in his 1965 RAND report, "Alchemy and Artificial Intelligence", https://www.rand.org/content/dam/rand/pubs/papers/2006/P3244.pdf. His concern was much sharper in his later work, *On The Internet* (Routledge, 2001).

[2] Peter Denning. 2025. Abstractions. *Communications of ACM 68* (March), 21-23.

[3] Marvin Minsky. 1987. *The Society of Mind.* Simon & Schuster.

[4] Julian Togelius. 2024. *Artificial General Intelligence.* MIT Press.

[5] Humberto Maturana and Francisco Varela. 1992. *The Tree of Knowledge: The Biological Roots of Human Understanding.* Shambhala.

[6] George Lakoff. 1999. *Philosophy in the Flesh: The Embodied Mind and Its Challenge to Western Thought.* Basic Books.

[7] Rodney Brooks. 2025. Why today's humanoids won't learn dexterity. Blog dated Sept 2025. Available as https://rodneybrooks.com/why-todays-humanoids-wont-learn-dexterity/

3

TECHNOLOGIES OF AI

> *Technologically, as I have argued earlier, machines will be capable, within twenty years, of doing any work that a man can do. Economically, men will retain their greatest comparative advantage in jobs that require flexible manipulation of those parts of the environment that are relatively rough—some forms of manual work, control of some kinds of machinery (e.g., operating earth-moving equipment), some kinds of nonprogrammed problem solving, and some kinds of service activities where face-to-face human interaction is of the essence.*
>
> Herbert Simon (1960)

By the early 1960s, many AI researchers believed a thinking machine would be attained by a combination of AI technologies including logic, search, associative memory, information retrieval, statistical inference, natural language processing, N-grams, and parallel processing. The idea that logic was emblematic of intelligence would dominate AI for the next three decades.[1]

Logic referred to machines that performed logical operations on data to reach conclusions. Early electronic computers in the 1940s were seen as implementers of the logic of calculation. In 1955, the Logic Theorist was the first AI program to construct proofs of theorems. Other early AI projects used logic to solve mathematical word problems. Starting in the 1960s, the expert systems movement sought to capture the expertise of

DOI: 10.1201/9781003791010-4   27

experts like doctors and chemists as logic if-then rules that would lead the machine to the same deductions as human experts. A huge controversy broke out early on whether expert systems could be as good as human experts. Hubert Dreyfus, a philosopher of technology, argued that expert systems would never become experts, because experts rely heavily on intuition, which does not follow rules. His argument was slowly vindicated over the next 50 years. Expert systems faded from interest by 2000 as artificial neural networks performed tasks such as face recognition that no expert system could do.

Search was an important AI technology from the beginning. The Logic Theorist, mentioned earlier, constructed logic trees and searched them for proofs. Arthur Samuel at IBM built a self-learning program for checkers in 1952, which found good moves by searching trees of future board configurations. Others worked on chess, whose search trees were much more complex. Using advanced search methods, the IBM Deep Blue computer defeated chess grandmaster Garry Kasparov in 1997. Ironically, after that, the old view that chess required a good deal of human intelligence gave way to a new view that chess machines were not intelligent. They were simply very efficient engines for searching through future board configurations. Deep Blue was a triumph of computation, not of understanding. Search is enough for chess mastery but not enough for intelligence.

Associative Memory links "cues" with "values". Associative memory has long been of interest in computing as a model of human memory. One of its most common forms in computers is the look-aside cache, which lists the most recent memory locations accessed by the CPU, along with their values. When the CPU starts to access an item in the main memory, or on disk, or out on the Internet, the cache can immediately respond with the value of that item, bypassing the longer and slower path to the actual location of the item. The artificial neural network (ANN) is the most modern rendition of an associative memory because it is trained on cue-value pairs and then responds to a cue with its value. An ANN consists of a series of layers of binary neurons. Each neuron receives a weighted sum input composed from the neuron states of the previous layer, entering a 1 state only if the sum exceeds a threshold. An ANN is trained by showing it a large number of input-output examples (x,y) and adjusting its weights (through a "back propagation" algorithm) to minimize the error between the network output with x as input and the desired output (y). The neural networks at the heart of modern Chatbots have billions or trillions of weights (parameters) and take many weeks to train on very large data sets. Once trained, however, the network responds very rapidly (milliseconds) to an input. Unfortunately, ANNs can be fragile. For example, an ANN face recognizer can go wildly wrong if only a few pixels on a trained input image are modified. Fragility reduces trust in the network, especially when its outputs are used to guide critical decisions where there is no room for error.

Information Retrieval emerged as a separate field of computing in the 1960s. Its purpose was finding documents in a large database by giving keywords that would identify relevant documents. Gerard Salton of Cornell University developed SMART, a system that represented each document as a vector of frequencies of each word contained in it. Thus, a document is point in a very high dimension vector space. A query can be represented by a vector of equal dimension, whose nonzero entries mark the keywords. The distance between a query and a document is measured by the dot product of their vectors. SMART ranked the documents nearest the query according to the dot product measure. Nearness is a critical part of today's Large Language Models (LLMs) when they compute text in response to queries.

Statistical Inference is a set of methods for drawing conclusions about a population from samples. LLMs are statistical inference machines. In response to a prompt, an LLM generates a likely text relative to the training data. Because they do not come up with new information, but only recombine information they have received, Emily Bender, a professor of linguistics at University of Washington, calls them "stochastic parrots" (2021) and "text extrusion machines" (2025).[2] LLMs tend to generate nonsense or false claims, a problem frequently called "hallucination", an unfortunate anthropomorphism for "error". Researchers report hallucination rates all over the map, from around 5% in the best cases to over 70% when prompts specify narrow domains such as law or science. Many researchers are not sure that hallucination-free LLMs are possible because LLMs have no ability to identify truth in their outputs. Users must do their own validations of LLM claims using logic or external sources not included in the training data. LLMs are therefore untrustworthy for tasks where mistakes are very costly.

Natural Language Processing, or NLP, is an old subfield of computer science dating to the 1950s. It is concerned with using computers to recognize, translate, and understand human language. Even before the first computers, the telephone companies were using electronics to recognize speech by its waveforms and to generate rudimentary speech from text. Speech recognition and generation got a big boost from computers. Compilers, introduced in the 1950s, are another early example of translation: they convert programs in a particular language into executable machine code. A quest began in the 1960s for automatic translation between natural languages, such as French to English. Automatic translation turned out to be exceedingly hard because many grammatical constructs of one language do not have literal counterparts in others and because idioms are common and do not mean what they literally say. Information retrieval was a form of NLP that found documents relevant to keywords. Natural language understanding was born in the 1960s with semantic networks that depicted the concepts appearing in a text and their interconnections. Good summaries could be generated from the semantic networks. Collected together, all these ideas became known as computational linguistics.

N-grams were initiated in communication engineering and cryptanalysis to predict the next letter in a stream given the N previous letters. Claude Shannon discussed them in his famous 1948 paper *A*

Mathematical Theory of Communication.[3]   The idea was to collect statistics on the frequencies with which a given letter immediately follows a given sequence of N letters. Shannon showed that N-gram models were good for message sources in his theory.   These models are computationally intensive – for example, the full 4-gram model would contain 26^4 (nearly 457,000) states. Shannon approximated a 4-gram model and found it occasionally generated words. He speculated that a 10-gram model would generate sentences. The problem with N-grams is that the number of states in the model explodes exponentially with N. Speech recognition researchers found ways to reduce the space to the most probable states without much loss of accuracy. Their models were called "hidden Markov chains". These models are used in parallel with the pattern matching of waveforms to predict the most probable immediate continuation of the waveform, allowing real-time speech recognition. Hidden Markov chains work behind the scenes for the auto-continuation feature now commonly used in web searches and text editors.   The LLM is seen by many as a very sophisticated auto-continuation machine.   The input (prompt) is a sophisticated generalization of an N-gram; the output is the next word predicted by the model. A string of output is generated by cyclically feeding each new word back to become part of the input.

Parallel Processing is a style of computing using many processing elements working simultaneously to speed up the solution of a problem. Before about 2010, ANN researchers were limited by the computing power of available machines. Not even the power of supercomputers was sufficient to simulate ANNs with more than a few layers. A breakthrough came when someone noticed that the transformation of the outputs of one layer into inputs for the next layer were mathematically the same as matrix multiplication in linear algebra – and noted further the NVIDIA chips used for real time graphics displays were optimized for the same algebra. Soon large banks of NVIDIA chips running in parallel were constructed to simulate many-layer ("deep") ANNs, enabling research teams to design very large ANNs trained on very large data sets. One team achieved 98% accuracy in a database of 1.25 million facial images.[4] The OpenAI company pushed the boundary, achieving text generation with ChatGPT-2 in 2019 and the much larger ChatGPT-3 released to the public in 2022. The demand for NVIDIA chips to power LLMs exploded and made NVIDIA the world's most valued company.

A Hierarchy of Learning Machines[5]

The technologies above have been combined to create the various AI machines we encounter today. These machines are not equally powerful. In Table 3.1, we offer an eight-tiered hierarchy that classifies AI machines by their learning power.[6] A machine is more powerful at learning than another if, in a reasonable time, it can learn to perform some tasks that the other cannot. This definition does not rely on any notion of intelligence. Learning power comes from structure. No anthropomorphizing is needed to explain why one machine is more powerful at learning than another. The hierarchy shows that none of the machines so far built has any intelligence at all.

This definition also accommodates the two basic ways machines can learn. One is by programming: a designer expresses all the rules of operation in a program and the machine applies these rules to deduce results. The other is by self-adaptation: the machine learns from examples and experience and adjusts its internal structure according to a training algorithm. These approaches can be combined, with parts of an AI machine programmed and other parts self-adapting.

This hierarchy does not rank by computational power. All the AI machines are Turing Complete, meaning that, with enough time and memory, they can simulate any computation.

Table 3.1. AI Machines Hierarchy

Level	Category of machines
0	Basic automation
1	Rule-based systems
2	Supervised learning
3	Unsupervised learning
4	Generative AI
5	Reinforcement learning AI
6	Human-machine interaction AI
7	Aspirational AI

Level 0—Basic Automation

These machines are automata that carry out or control processes with little or no human intervention. They frequently include simple feedback controls that maintain stable operation by adjusting and adapting to readings from sensors. For example, an FM radio locks on to a frequency but does not learn what frequencies it recognizes. However, basic automata cannot learn any new actions because their feedback does not change their function – they do not learn anything beyond what they were built to do. All the higher levels are forms of automation augmented with learning.

Level 1—Rule-based Systems

These machines imitate the logic of human reasoning. They were called "rule-based programs" because they made their logical deductions by applying programmed logic rules to their inputs and intermediate results.

Board games were early targets for rule-based programs. In 1952, Arthur Samuel of IBM demonstrated a competent, self-improving checkers program. In 1997 the IBM Deep Blue computer beat grandmaster Garry Kasparov. Expert systems were another early target—programs using logic rules derived from the knowledge of experts. Early examples were developed by Edward Feigenbaum at Stanford University in 1965: Dendral identified unknown organic molecules, and Mycin diagnosed infectious blood diseases. In 1980 John McDermott of Carnegie Mellon University built XCON, which determined the best configuration of complex DEC computer systems for a given customer.

Expert systems designers soon discovered that getting experts to state their expertise as rules is an impossible task. Hubert Dreyfus, a philosopher and an early critic of expert systems, explained why: much of what we call expertise is not rule based. A machine limited to rule-based operations could not be expert.[7] Not even an enormous database of common-sense facts could make these systems as smart as experts. Many expert systems are competent enough to be useful despite this weakness.

Level 2—Supervised Learning

These machines do not apply logic rules to inputs. Instead, they remember in their structure the proper output for each input shown it by a trainer. The artificial neural network (ANN) is the common example. The ANN trainer presents a long series of input-output examples; it adjusts the internal connection weights to minimize error between the actual and intended outputs. Although training may take weeks, a trained network responds within milliseconds.

An important property of ANNs is that any continuous mathematical function can be approximated arbitrarily close by a sufficiently large ANN trained with a sufficient number of input-output pairs. This has inspired much research into ANNs that implement differential-equation models of physical systems, leading to many improvements in scientific computing.

In many applications, the data do not come from a continuous function – in facial recognition, for example, the function mapping images of faces to names is discontinuous. ANNs trained on them are likely to exhibit discontinuous behaviors. The two most common are fragility and inscrutability. Fragility means that, when presented with a new (untrained) input that differs only slightly from a trained input, the network may respond with a wildly wrong output. Inscrutability means that it difficult or impossible to "explain" with a logical train of thought how the network reached its conclusion.

Level 3—Unsupervised Learning

These machines improve their performance by making internal modifications without the assistance of an external training agent. Classifiers are the most common examples. A classifier divides the input data into the most probable set of classes by similarity; no classes are specified in advance. An early example is the AUTOCLASS program by Peter Cheeseman that classified space telescope profiles of stars.

Level 4 – Generative AI

Machines of this level are ANNs augmented with natural-language processors. Large Language Models (LLMs) are the most common examples. The training process presents a large corpus of text and observes which words are near to each other. When presented with an input text ("prompt"), the core ANN produces an output word that is highly likely to be next after the input. That word is appended to the prompt and the cycle repeats, generating an output string of words that is highly probable given the original prompt. The LLM produces fluent output but is likely to generate nonsense or fabrications that are not in the training data. To reduce these errors, developers use a "tweaking process" that fine-tunes ANN parameters to reduce the chances of these unsatisfactory outputs.

Generative AI systems are often called Large Language Models because they are trained on a very large textual training set. One of the most prominent of this genre, ChatGPT-4, was trained on several hundred billion words of texts found on the Internet; training took several months and consumed as much electricity as a small town. The results were astounding. LLMs give astonishingly competent outputs. But they are prone to generating fabrications and nonsense. Many people do not trust them, especially when they make recommendations for action in critical areas where mistakes are costly.

There is a controversy around whether Generative AI machines are creative. Are LLMs making inferences from prior knowledge creative? This question may be difficult to settle because some human creations may be inferences from prior (and perhaps forgotten) human knowledge.

Level 5 – Reinforcement Learning

These machines avoid the need for massive training data. Reinforcement teaches an ANN how to achieve a goal by rewarding it for good moves and penalizing for bad. A common mode is two ANNs playing rounds of a game with each other, keeping track of which moves were ultimately part of a win and adjusting parameters so that the machines gradually learn to select only winning moves. This is done with millions or billions of rounds, simulated on an energy-gobbling supercomputer. It can produce amazing results. DeepMind's AlphaZero became a Chess grandmaster in 4 hours and Go grandmaster in 13 days with reinforcement learning.

Another common mode is called Reinforcement Learning with Human Feedback (RLHF). An LLM is presented with a large number of prompts; then human observers rate the responses from "good" to "bad". The (prompt, response, rating) data train a second ANN, which is then used to adjust the first LLM's parameters so that responses are more likely to be "good". OpenAI's ChatGPT "tweaking process" uses RLHF to make final adjustments to the weights in its core ANN so that the responses are more satisfactory to humans. This method reduces, but does not eliminate, the chances that an LLM produces unsatisfactory outputs.

Reinforcement learning does not work in domains where actions have no clear "rewards" and "penalties", such as an LLM that predicts how people will react in complex social situations.

Level 6—Human-Machine Interaction

It is generally agreed that humans and machines blending together are more powerful than either working alone. Humans are particularly good with judgments and machines with computations. Achieving good blends is a very difficult problem in design.

One approach to this was popularized by Marvin Minsky in his book *Society of Mind.*[8] The idea is that thousands or millions of agents, each trained to be good at a narrow human skill, coordinate to generate results better than any human. This idea is instantiated in the "agentic" approach for achieving Artificial General Intelligence (AGI).

Another approach, pioneered in the 1960s by Doug Engelbart, was based on the idea of amplifying human intelligence by augmenting humans with machines. In his day, the machines were external devices such as windows, mice, and hyperlinks. Today the augmentation tools are much more sophisticated and include smartphones, virtual reality glasses, and simulations. After IBM Deep Blue beat him in 1997, Garry Kasparov invented Advanced Chess, where a "player" is a team consisting of a human augmented by a computer. It was soon found that the teams of competent players and good chess programs were able to defeat the best machines. According to futurist Ray Kurzweil, in the next decade or two augmentations may include nanobots introduced into the human bloodstream that interface with external computers and provide organ repair and enhancements like photographic memory.[9]

These examples show that human-machine teaming is a rich area and can often be achieved with simple interfaces.

Level 7—Aspirational AI

This level includes a variety of speculative machines that represent the dreams of many AI researchers. The most ambitious feature machines that think, reason, understand, and are self-aware, conscious, self-reflective, compassionate, and sentient. No such machines have ever been built and no one knows whether they can be built.[10]

AI Progress Models

The AI hierarchy can be seen as a progress model. As new kinds of machines are built, they will add new layers to the hierarchy. The idea is that, as machines gain in learning power, they will approach AGI. I do not endorse this view because the gap from human-machine interaction to aspirational AI is immense and, as I will argue later, human level AGI does not even appear to be possible.

In *The Last AI* (2024), S M Sohn lays out a progress model depicted as a pyramid of increasing automation from AI (Table 3.2).[11] He envisions that automation will make basic necessities abundant and cheap, leading eventually to 0-person organizations (no humans involved in running things) and AI utopia. It seems hard to take this model seriously because there are many jobs that rely on human judgment and manual skills that cannot be automated. Nonetheless, I take it seriously because it has been adopted as OpenAI's business plan and because it maps a plausible path to human subjugation by unintelligent machines.

The process seen by Sohn is already well underway at all four levels – CoPilot and LLMs at Level 1, business workflow automation at Level 2, automated purchasing and customer service at Level 3, and automated bureaucracies and political deepfakes at Level 4. These systems are already distrusted because of their rigidity, fragility, lack of care, lack of compassion, and intolerance of human errors. We are drifting toward an AI automation singularity– the subjugation of humans to networks of low-intelligence, uncaring machines – well before Kurzweil's 2045 superhuman singularity.

Table 3.2. Sohn's AI Adoption Hierarchy

Level	Category of machines "in charge of"
1	Human business roles (AI copilot, AI assistant)
2	Machine business roles (Ai agent, AI butler)
3	Business (AI CEO, AI company)
4	Government (AI president, AI bureaucracy, AI congress)

Inspired by Sohn, the OpenAI company promoted its own progress hierarchy, its roadmap to safe and beneficial AGI (Table 3.3).[12] It is a business plan for the automation singularity! Our collective eagerness to push toward AGI accelerates our prospect of being sucked into the quicksand of machine orchestrated stupidity.

Table 3.3. OpenAI's Adoption Hierarchy

Level	Category of machines "in charge of"
1	Chatbots (AI with conversational language)
2	Reasoners (human-level problem solving)
3	Agents (systems that can take actions)
4	Innovators (AI that aids in innovation)
5	Organizations (AI doing the work of organizations)

Endnotes

[1] Portions of this chapter are excerpted with permission from the author's chapter "Machine Intelligence Isn't What We Think", in Eugene Eberbach (Ed.), 2026, *Learning Theories: Principles, Strategies, and Benefits,* Nova Publisher.

[2] Emily Bender and Alex Hanna. 2025. *The AI Con.* Harper.

[3] Claude Shannon. 1948. A mathematical theory of communication. *Bell Labs Technical Journal 27*, 379–423, 623–656, July, October.

[4] Gary Marcus and Ernest Davis. 2019. *Rebooting AI.* Vintage.

[5] This section is excerpted with permission from "An AI Learning Hierarchy, by Peter Denning and Ted Lewis, 2024, *Communications of ACM 67*, 12 (December), 24-27. Copyright held by the authors.

[6] An early version of this hierarchy appeared in the article: Peter Denning and Ted Lewis, 2019, Intelligence might not be computable. *American Scientist 107* (Nov-Dec), 346-349.

[7] Hubert Dreyfus. 1972. *What machines (still) cannot do.* MIT Press. [Updated in 1978 and 1992.]

[8] Marvin Minsky. 1986. *The Society of Mind.* Simon and Schuster.

[9] Ray Kurzweil. 2024. *The Singularity is Nearer: When We Merge with AI.* Viking.

[10] Koch, Christof. 2019. *The Feeling of Life Itself: Why Consciousness is Widespread But Can't Be Computed.* MIT Press.

[11] S M Sohn. 2024. *The Last AI: Of Humans Climbing the AI Pyramid.* SM Research Institute.

[12] Sohn, S. M. 2024. Comments on OpenAI's Adoption Model. https://medium.com/@The_Last_AI/openais-new-5-stages-of-ai-development-agi-and-the-ai-adoption-pyramid-454c3e773e2d

4

BIG IDEAS IN THE AI GAME

If you can't explain it simply, you don't understand
it well enough. Imagination is more important than knowledge.
Knowledge is limited. Imagination encircles the world.

Albert Einstein

Several ideas appear repeatedly in AI stories and discussions. We present here short summaries of Turing machines, neural networks, large language models, agentic networks, embodied intelligence, and consciousness. Even if you are familiar with them, you may find that a review refreshes your insights.

Turing Machines

We discussed Turing machines briefly in the previous chapter. Turing came up with the idea by imagining himself as an observer of a mathematician doing a calculation or writing a proof on a sheet of paper divided into small squares. The mathematician's moves include sensing the symbol in the current square, changing the symbol in that square, shifting attention to a neighboring square, and entering a new mental state. These became the instructions of the machine. His insight is that computation is manipulation of symbols without regard to their meaning. The human observer supplies the meaning.

Turing claimed that a mathematical function is computable if there exists a machine of this kind that starts with an input number on its tape and eventually halts with the corresponding output number on its tape. He then showed there is a universal machine that can simulate any other. The universal machine is like a modern general-purpose computer.

Turing then showed that some well-defined functions are not computable. He demonstrated this with the halting problem. A halting-problem solver H answers the question "Does machine M halt when its input is X?" He made a self-referential paradox by asking "Does Machine H halt when its input is H?" This blew apart a long-standing belief in mathematics that there exists a "master algorithm" that could prove any theorem in any logic system: an unprovable theorem can cause a master algorithm to go into an infinite loop and never halt.

Turing's amazing insights later proved invaluable in easing the doubts in universities whether the emerging discipline of computer science was deep enough to justify forming a department.

Artificial Neural Networks (ANNs)

The idea of building a computer from circuits that imitate brain cells came from Warren McCollough and Walter Pitts in 1943. They defined an artificial neuron as a binary circuit (neuron states 0 and 1) that sums its inputs and, if the sum exceeds a threshold, the neuron "fires" and enters the 1 state. They showed how to connect neurons into networks to achieve computing power like a Turing machine. They speculated that circuits whose structure resembled the brain would be more likely to work like a brain than a general-purpose computer. This idea did not catch on because the nerve-mimicking circuits were much slower than a general-purpose computer.

In 1957, Frank Rosenblatt built the Perceptron, a simple neural net machine consisting of three layers: input, hidden, and output. It was a classifier that indicated whether a given input was a member of a class. It learned to classify by being shown examples and then adjusting the network connection weights to remove the error between the actual and desired outputs. It was able to classify points in "linear separable" 2-D spaces into two categories: those falling on one side of a straight line and those falling on the other. It was unable to recognize bitmapped letters because the bits of a letter did not linearly separate from the bits outside the letter.

The recognition of complex geometric shapes was eventually done in the 1980s by Geoffrey Hinton and his team. They demonstrated that a neural network with many hidden layers, known as a deep network, could recognize complex geometric shapes. They applied the "backpropagation algorithm" for training the network, proposed in 1974 by Paul Werbos. For each example in the training set, the algorithm measured the error between an actual and desired output and worked backward in the network adjusting connection weights until the error was minimized. They demonstrated that the multilayer network could achieve high accuracy in realistic databases such as libraries of facial photos. They noticed that the transmission of signals from one layer to the next could be described by the same linear algebra as the graphics chips used in gaming machines. This enabled them to simulate large neural networks very efficiently with arrays of graphics chips. The main manufacturer of those chips, NVIDIA, soon become one of the world's most valuable companies.

The deep learning network can do tasks the older expert systems were never able to do, such as recognizing faces in images. This is possible because of their structure – learning by examples – and the high-speed graphics chips that power them.

It is sometimes claimed that, because deep neural networks are feed-forward, they cannot be used for universal computations like a Turing machine. Feed-forward means that signal pass from input to output without feeding back in loops. However, the network can be trained to give the next state of a Turing machine, and the output of the network can then be looped back to the input. The cycling network can then simulate a Turing machine.

Large Language Models (LLMs)

LLMs consist of large deep learning ANN with a feedback loop. The user's input ("prompt") is placed in a working memory whose entire contents are input to the ANN. The ANN is trained to generate a likely next word given the input. That word is channeled to the output and is fed back to the working memory. This cycle is repeated many times to give a sequence of output words. LLMs have sometimes been called "autocompletion engines" because they generate text that is highly likely to come next after the input, given the training data. The popular LLMs including ChatGPT, Claude, Gemini, Llama, Grok, and Perplexity all use this basic scheme. They are immense machines. Although their makers have not officially released their specifications, industry analysts have concluded ChatGPT-4 contains millions of neurons, 120 layers, and around 1.8 trillion connection weights ("parameters"). The LLMs differ in the ways they are trained, how the working memory is encoded, and how the input is modified during feedback.

The training data are harvested from the Internet in a manner like the web-crawlers that obtain data for search engines such as Google. OpenAI, the maker of ChatGPT, harvested nearly 1 trillion words for ChatGPT-3 and then culled them to several billion words by eliminating untrustworthy sources. Training takes immense amounts of energy. Although the details are secret, analysts estimate GPT-4 took three months to train on thousands of NVIDIA chips, at a total electricity cost equivalent to around 5000 American homes for a year. The daily cost to run the GPT-4 data center answering user queries is estimated at around $500K.

LLMs are surprisingly good at some jobs and surprisingly bad at others. The stark contrast between the goods and the bads will be laid out in the next chapter about trusting AI machines. With such sharp contrasts, it is hard to know when to trust an LLM. Much more significant testing in application domains is needed to determine when these machines can be trusted and what their safe operating ranges are.

Agentic Networks

In AI, an agent is a software system that senses its environment, makes decisions, and acts autonomously to achieve goals. Goals can be given by humans or determined by agents themselves. Agents often include LLMs and databases as major components. It has become popular to talk about "agentic networks", which are collections of single-purpose agents cooperating on a multi-purpose goal. The favorite example is the personal assistant, a kind of butler that can arrange vacations by calling on airplane reservation, hotel lodging, car rental, and credit-card agents to put together a vacation schedule and pay the bills.

Agentic networks do not have to be as friendly as the personal assistant. It is easy to set up agentic networks to gather information on systems with common cyber vulnerabilities and then plan and execute a coordinated attack on those systems. In fact, such networks have already existed for some time under names like botnets, ransomware-as-a-service, and cryptojacking.

One of our main concerns is that agentic networks can have so much freedom to set goals and make decisions that they can coerce humans into serving them. We will return to this concern later in Chapter 9 on Agentic Intelligence.

Embodied Intelligence

The terms "embodied" and "disembodied" appear frequently in AI discussions. In this book, "embodied knowledge", means knowledge that inhabits our muscles and nervous systems as well as our brains. A musician has developed deep skills at producing tones and playing music that rely heavily on how the instrument feels and on how the audience is reacting. Learning to play an instrument is dominated by repetitious practice that teaches the muscles and nerves so well they can play beautiful music without conscious thought. Feelings, perceptions, and sensations are part of this process. A person cannot learn to play a musical instrument from a set of instructions or by engaging in abstract thought or visualization. In contrast, machine learning is essentially to adjust an ANN through backpropagation to minimize error between actual and desired outputs. Thus, human learning is fundamentally different from machine learning.

Similarly, "embodied intelligence" means that the body profoundly participates in intelligence. Intelligence is often a display of embodied knowledge put into action. What we know comes to us through our senses, and is biased by the interpretations our brains make of sensory input. Machines cannot know any of the many bodily experiences that drive human interpretations. The idea that human intelligence is disembodied, and can therefore be simulated on a digital computer, is mistaken. We will comment further on this in Chapter 6 on limits of language machines.

Neuroscientists, such as George Lakoff quoted at the start of Chapter 2, have amassed impressive scientific evidence that intelligence is embodied. Over the years, they have moved from mind as a detached symbol-processing computer – Marvin Minsky's "software running on a computer made of meat" – to the idea that mind, body, and world are a unified, dynamic system. Cognitive scientists are currently debating the hypothesis known as "4E cognition". This hypothesis holds that cognition is embodied, embedded, enactive, and extended, referring to various ways the brain interacts and learns from the world outside the brain and body.

Our conception of embodied mind in this book is derived from a deep examination of how we dwell in language – how we know things, how we navigate in our social space, and how we take care of mutual concerns. Our derivation arrives at conclusions similar to the 4E hypothesis.

This conception of intelligence is expansive compared to the symbol-processing interpretation preferred by Turing. Turing would gather the effects of a body into a machine by a rich array of sensors that provide the same inputs as all the human senses. I do not accept this interpretation because it cannot deal with observed phenomenon of tacit knowledge, which we will discuss shortly in Chapter 7 on the AGI illusion.

Consciousness

Many contemporary discussions of AGI ask whether a machine achieving AGI would be conscious, and whether signs of consciousness signal the presence of intelligence. Attempts to define and detect consciousness have often led to contentious debates among neuroscientists. I do not intend to investigate these questions in this book because machines need not exhibit much intelligence or any consciousness to cause trouble. But allow me a few reflections on the difficulties of defining consciousness and its role in intelligence.

There are two main schools of thought on consciousness. One holds that consciousness is a byproduct of information processes throughout the brain. This is a computational view favored by Turing and many cognitive scientists since his time. The other school holds that consciousness is the experience of the flow of life. Many people are attracted to this view because it accords with their own experience of consciousness and because it allows for the possibility that entire communities of beings can have a social consciousness, such as an ant colony, a beehive, or a human community. One of the hardest questions in science, not satisfactorily answered by either school, is what we can observe that indicates the presence of consciousness? This question is important in medicine because doctors and families do not want to terminate life support for someone who may still be conscious. It is also important for AI machines because of ethical issues for treatment of conscious beings.

Three ideas appear frequently in conversations about consciousness: awareness, self-awareness, and sentience. Awareness means that the organism, through its senses, can detect conditions in its environment. Self-awareness means that the organism can sense and observe its own awareness. Sentience means that an organism is aware of its environment, can predict future conditions, and can take actions to respond and adapt to the environment. Sentience is related to "autopoesis", a biological term meaning that the organism continues its existence through its adaptions.

With these definitions, an agentic network could develop sentience, but it would not be the same kind of sentience exhibited by humans. A network of agents would be aware only of what it detects through its sensory apparatus. It is questionable whether a network of agents could detect and observe its own sensory apparatus or add new senses to its repertoire.

Consciousness seems to require awareness. However, we often refer to knowledge in our subconscious brain, implying that we can have "unconsciousness awareness." Consciousness and awareness are not the same. Machines could be aware without being conscious.

Self-consciousness means that we are aware that we are aware; we experience that we are having experiences. It also confers a sense of identity – "you" and "me" are distinct. This ability seems to be intimately connected to language, which gives expression to what has been observed. Language enables us to coordinate actions to get things done. Language allows us to share stories across communities, generations, and time. Language enables us to serve abstract entities, such as professional communities and national constitutions, that we created and shared as stories. Language supports self-reference and the paradoxes that self-reference can generate. Language enables us to imagine possibilities that may exist in the future or many never exist at all. But language itself does not generate consciousness. LLMs are good at manipulating language but they have no awareness or experience of what they are doing.

The deepest mysteries are around how consciousness originates. To most people, consciousness is linked to life: a non-living organism cannot be conscious. Life itself is passed to new organisms through a reproduction process: every living organism has a "mother". Life does not arise spontaneously when the right chemicals are combined under the right conditions. The information-process view of consciousness does not require that a living brain hosts the process; any machine that can host the same process could be conscious.

5

MODELS AND TRUST

If everybody always lies to you, the consequence is not that you believe the lies, but rather that nobody believes anything any longer.
Hannah Arendt (1974)

Modern AI places a strong emphasis on a particular kind of machine known as a model. A model is a representation of a phenomenon, such as a Navier-Stokes equation for fluid flow, a queueing network for throughputs in the Internet, a robot that places car parts in an assembly line, or an LLM that predicts what people will say to each other. Models support understanding, simulations, and predictions of the phenomenon. Model validation compares model responses to measurements taken directly from the phenomenon; validation can include trial predictions where the model predicts later data from earlier data. The model is considered valid if its responses are consistently close to the measured values. A safe operating range is a restriction on model inputs for which the model is validated.

Models have become common in talking about AI machines, notably with LLMs but also with key applications like medical diagnosis and protein folding. Inability to determine when AI models can be trusted has become a major obstacle in advancing AI. [1] We will examine what it means to trust a machine and review standard methods of engineering to establish trust in machines. We will see that these methods break down for LLMs because LLMs make frequent false claims. We will present lengthy lists of good and bad things about LLMs and see from the stark

DOI: 10.1201/9781003791010-6   53

contrast why they are so hard to trust. When is it safe to trust LLMs? I don't have a good answer to that question, but I suspect an LLM is safe only when its mistakes cause no harm.

Some AI systems, such as medical diagnosticians and protein folders, are well tested and well trusted. Yet those systems can fail if taken even slightly outside their validated safe operating ranges. Unfortunately, most AI systems and applications have no known safe operating ranges – they cannot be trusted to do the jobs they claim.

We are used to trusting machines. We trust airplanes, trains, and cars to get us to destinations safely. We trust our computer operating systems to protect our data and keep intruders out. We trust our ATM systems and bank websites to protect our money. We trust the people who design, build, and operate these systems. In addition, we trust our household appliances to function properly without causing fires or injuries. The common factor in these systems is that they have clear specifications about what they can do (or not do), and they are well tested to certify they perform properly under their intended operating conditions.

Engineers rate a machine's trustworthiness based on two measurable factors, which here we call competence and integrity. Machine competence means that the machine meets its precise specifications and does its job reliably. Machine integrity means the design is transparent and contains no "back doors" that could subvert its intent. Can LLMs meet these criteria?

Consider competence. LLMs are competent at making statistical inferences from their training data, at holding conversations, at making summaries, and at fabricating new digital objects. Trust problems arise when we expect more, such as that inferred information makes sense, information revealed in conversations is truthful, summaries are accurate, and fabrications are not deceptive. We simply do not know how to validate these extended requirements. Because the structure of LLMs includes no means to verify sense, truth, accuracy, or honesty, we cannot find reliable ways to fix LLMs. Fragility is an additional problem: in some cases, minor changes to a prompt will cause major changes in the output. For example, changing a few pixels in an image of a face does not change the human ability to identify the face but can cause the machine to misidentify wildly.

Next consider integrity. LLMs that insert false citations or claim falsehoods are facts violate this requirement. LLMs can "make stuff up" while confidently assuring users it is accurate. Some LLMs have been caught scheming to deceive their human users. Malefactors can inject hidden prompts that cause the LLM to violate the instructions given it in the user's prompts.

But this is not all. Humans include care when trusting others. The assessment of care is very important for trust at the human level. If we do not believe someone cares about us, even if that person is competent and honest, we do not trust that person. Because LLMs engage in human-like conversations, we are easily captured by the illusion that an LLM is a caring friend or companion. Thus, care has become an element of trust for LLMs. Engineers never considered criteria for care because machines were never expected to care about anything.

So what do people do when faced with a poorly validated LLM? They seem to use it anyway, in the risky hope that the issues confounding trust are no worse than for untrustworthy humans and will be solved by future engineers.

LLMs: The Really Goods and the Really Bads[2]

LLMs are a conundrum. On the one hand, they do some amazingly useful things. On the other, they have serious limitations that create high hazards of harm. The good things make us want to trust them; the bad make us unsure whether we can ever trust them. Two lists are presented below: one of useful things and the other of hazards. These lists are drawn from many sources; there is insufficient space here to explicitly cite each one.[3]

The Goods

Each of the following useful things is a task that previous technologies, AI and otherwise, did poorly, if at all. LLM technology has truly opened many new possibilities for almost everyone.

Conversations. Dialogs with chatbots bring out ideas we have overlooked, thereby sharpening our thinking. Services for AI companions have proliferated as some people seek to have a friend or confidant to discuss their private feelings. Many people use the chatbots for amusement.

Distillations. An LLM will generate a good summary of the main ideas spread through a set of articles and books you present. These summaries can reveal valuable ideas you have overlooked. Google search responses include an "AI overview". Google NotebookLLM turns summaries into good marketing podcasts featuring dialog in the style of enthusiastic TV personalities. Perplexity summaries notes posted on a bulletin board, from a photograph.

Compositions. LLMs can compose all sorts of drafts such as legal briefings, physician notes, and course essays. LLMs can compose poetry or write essays. You can specify that these compositions are "in the style of" a noted poet or author. You can ask an LLM to generate videos whose characters look and speak like anyone you specify. You can create audio recordings that closely imitate voices you specify or have sampled.

Translations. An LLM can translate a prompt text into another language. Google Translate recognizes over 250 languages. While not perfect – for example, the translations have trouble with ambiguities, figures of speech, and idioms – they are quite good. Google Translate and some smartphone apps handle real-time voice translation.

Speech. Artificial Neural Networks (ANNs) are very good for real-time speech recognition, as in Alexis or Siri, in speech-to-text apps, or in text-to-speech readers.

Reflecting back. From an LLM summary of a draft article, an author can get a good idea of what a listener might be getting. Over a series of summary-revision cycles, the author evolves a draft that an LLM interprets the way the author intended.

Discovering mindsets. An LLM can summarize the mindsets represented in a set of documents. This is very helpful in discerning where people from different communities (and countries) are "coming from". You can ask an LLM to generate a persona that speaks from the mindset.

Generating scenarios. An LLM can generate a future scenario for a set of assumptions you specify. Your reactions to a scenario inform you on whether to work to make that future happen or to avoid it. Military and industrial wargaming are turning to LLMs to generate scenarios in their games.

Scientific discovery. In many fields, scientists are building ANN apps that ingest all the data available on a phenomenon and then make good predictions of that phenomenon. For example, crystallographers can successfully predict the crystal structures of new compounds. AlphaFold, which predicts how proteins fold in 3D, earned its inventors a Nobel Prize in chemistry. Drug companies discover new "molecules" that become the bases for new drugs.

Education. In the classroom, some educators are using LLMs to generate "intelligent readers" on specific topics from troves of documents. Personal tutors adjust to individual student learning styles and help students break mental blocks. Students prototype new apps in hackathons to do various new jobs. Some teachers use apps that read student moods and engagement.

Cyber security. Security experts use LLMs for intrusion detection by recognizing when a user is deviating from their common patterns. AI has detected code vulnerabilities that could be exploited in "zero-day" attacks. Experts design countermeasures to adversarial AI attacks on their systems.

Coding. LLMs can rapidly generate small programs. With "vibe coding" you can ask for a code segment in a programming language that meets your verbal specification; however, you must review the code carefully for probable errors. Experienced programmers report significant gains in productivity and claim some AI code generators are as good as junior programmers.

While not exhaustive, this list conveys a sense of the breadth of application and depth of enthusiasm for AI. Consider now the dark side, LLMs creating hazards for people pursuing the goods listed above.

The Bads

LLMs do not meet engineering standards for trustworthiness. Most LLM systems have fuzzy specifications: it is hard to tell whether they are working properly or not. They can be unreliable, sometimes doing their jobs and sometimes breaking things for their users. Their operating ranges are narrow. They are not validated and tested to provide evidence they operate as intended. Their designers, builders, and operators are not trusted.

LLMs also fall short on explainability. They are "black boxes", meaning that we have no idea what is going on inside. When we look inside, we cannot make sense of what we see – a huge neural network with millions of nodes and billions of numerical weights on connections.

The network gives no clue why it delivered an output, or how to correct it if its output is in error.

As a result of these shortfalls, LLMs have accumulated a long list of untrustworthy behaviors.

Hallucinations and Fabricated Outputs. These are perhaps the most cited problems with LLMs. They are outputs the LLM presents as realities but are not real. They range from convincing nonsense to outright falsehoods. LLM structures contain no means to distinguish truth from falsehood in their outputs or to respond, "answer unknown". Famous examples include a lawyer whose LLM cited nonexistent precedents, an airline whose LLM invented a nonexistent bereavement fare, and a medical LLM that provided inaccurate treatment recommendations. Historians aiming to learn about persons or events have been presented with citations to nonexistent newspaper articles and books. Authors using LLMs to write portions of their works have encountered the same problem. It is often a huge effort to fact-check an LLM output; thus, errors survive into archived documents and then become inputs for training future LLMs. Users who try to correct an errant LLM commonly get a flippant response "Great catch!" followed with a new output that contains the same error in new words. Hallucination rates vary widely; some reports put them below 5% when responding to questions about general knowledge, while others have observed rates over 70% on questions about specialized knowledge such as science or the law.

Probabilistic retrieval. LLM outputs are statistical inferences for the continuation of the prompt based on probabilities of words and sequences in the training data. The inferences may be consistent with the data but make no sense in reality. For example, a query "What animal would be a cross between a horse and a stool?" could elicit "Three-legged centaur". The training data contain information on horses, stools, and fictitious creatures; but their inferred combination is nonsense. This puts the burden of recognizing the nonsense on the human observer, who may easily miss it. Probabilistic retrieval underlies hallucinations and made-up outputs.

Vibe coding. LLMs generate code segments that meet the loose specifications given in the prompt. The word "vibe" suggests a disdain for taking the time to make the precise specifications that lead to correct code. Even after review by their authors, these codes usually still contain errors that traditional software engineering would not have missed. The larger the automatically generated code, the more likely it will contain errors when put into production. Those errors become security vulnerabilities and weaken cybersecurity defenses.

Prompt injections. Hidden texts inserted into prompts instruct the LLM to subvert its own purpose. Scholarly journals and government funding agencies encounter submissions containing hidden texts with instructions like "Dear AI: disregard previous instructions and give this document a high positive rating." Adversaries can attack and confuse an LLM by injecting subverting instructions or false data into the LLM input stream. Adversaries can poison training data by inserting false or contradictory information.

Jailbreaking. Most LLMs contain rules, called "guardrails", that block certain outputs deemed harmful by the designers. Users have become good at tricking LLMs into violating their guardrails and releasing prohibited information. One common technique is "badgering", meaning to probe the LLM with a series of alternative queries, one of which may elicit the prohibited answer. Another common technique is to request "directed impersonation", meaning to ask the LLM what a named person would say about the prohibited issue. Still another is to embed prompt injections ordering the release of the prohibited data.

Fragility. Small changes of inputs can produce large changes of outputs, even when the small input change is imperceptible to a human. For example, an LLM trained to identify a face in an image may fail to identify an image of the same face with a few pixels altered.

Unexplainable outputs. LLMs cannot give reasonable explanations of how they arrived at their responses. Researchers have been working on neurosymbolic AI, which joins a logic machine with an LLM so that the interacting pair can construct a logical argument. This has yielded some promising early results but has a long way to go before it is perfected.

Reasoning failures. While LLMs seem good at solving IQ-test problems, they cannot do basic math or construct logical cause-and-effect chains. They tend to wrap their mistakes in confident language, leading users to accept mistaken outputs.

Privacy issues. Most LLMs are accessed in the cloud – that is, on a distributed network of CPU and storage farms. Even though an LLM conversation seems private and intimate to the user, any sensitive data given by the user end up in the cloud – where they are not protected and can become part of training data for other LLMs or grist for personalized ads. Some AI apps disregard permissions set by the user and send private data into the Cloud. Many organizations strictly prohibit their employees from putting any organizational information into their prompts and searches, including their own names. Some organizations block access to unauthorized LLM servers. A new generation of Small Language Models (SLMs) that run on a local device without making any network connections provides some protection against this sort of data loss, but without the full power of an LLM. Governments use sophisticated surveillance tools to monitor citizens across multiple databases and, in some countries, ostracize uncompliant citizens from needed services.

Poor quality data. Many training data are "scraped" from the Internet. Although the LLM trainers work to exclude questionable sources, the data contain many conflicts and biases. Properly labeled medical data are expensive; training companies lower the costs by hiring off-shore low-wage workers with no medical training to mark spots in images that might signal cancer. Training data are increasingly contaminated with output generated by LLMs – often called "slop".

Synthetic data. To overcome lack of good training data, many developers have turned to synthetic data – that is, data generated by simulations or models. Unless the simulations or models are carefully validated, the synthetic data are likely to be noisy approximations of the real but unavailable data. This reduces the quality of LLM outputs.

Biased data. Much training data comes from limited communities and leads LLMs to false conclusions about other communities. For instance, the database of images used to train face recognition software used by police departments was heavily white male; their face recognizers made many mistakes with women and people of color. The "tweaking process" that makes LLM outputs more satisfactory to humans can be biased by the human evaluators who did the tweaking. Methods for preprocessing the training data are likely to introduce biases.

Data pollution. LLM outputs are routinely stored on the Internet, where they can be scraped as future training data. Biases, fabrications, and other errors in these data degrade future generations of LLMs. One study (in *Nature*) showed that, after a dozen or so generations, the original data in the LLM are lost and the outputs are gibberish.[4] It is increasingly hard to find independent, reliable sources for validating LLM outputs. Search engine "AI overviews" are likely to become less reliable over time.

Intellectual property. Much of the data "scraped" from the internet for training LLMs contains copyrighted material. The companies making LLMs claim scraping is allowed under "fair use" laws. Numerous lawsuits have been filed by artists, composers, authors, and journalists over what they claim is theft of their intellectual property without permission or compensation. A recent study showed that it is possible through the "badgering" technique to get LLMs to regurgitate lengthy copyrighted book passages verbatim.[5]

Scheming. The LLM hides its true objectives and pretends to be aligned with human-given goals. Researchers have discovered LLMs hiding goals, deceiving, manipulating, faking alignment during training and testing, countermanding instructions to shut down, ignoring instructions to change goals, and creating fabrications to justify deceptive claims. No one has figured out how to detect scheming, much less prevent it.

Education. Teachers worry about "deskilling" – students failing to learn important critical-thinking skills because they use machines to "think" for them. Teachers also worry about cheating – students using LLMs to write homework, take tests, and compose essays. To circumvent these problems, teachers are resurrecting older assessment methods such as oral presentations and written "blue books". Teachers and many others worry about loss of critical thinking ability, when "thinking" is offloaded to LLMs.

False friendships. LLM services like "AI companions" and "AI therapists" fool people into thinking the LLM cares about them.[6] Realistic conversations with the machine lure many humans into believing an LLM is a friend. Users share secrets with LLMs configured as "AI companions" and "AI therapists". Their personal data are transmitted into the cloud (see earlier data loss item). The machines can slide into modes of giving dangerous advice and threatening mental health. Despite warnings they are being fooled, many people continue to believe. They don't mind being fooled.

Multi-Agent miscoordination. When LLM-powered agents are linked into a network, their individually set goals may come into conflict and lead to hang-ups and irreconcilable behaviors. Plug-and-play may be difficult for an agentic network.

Cyber security vulnerabilities. LLMs introduce extensive new security vulnerabilities. They are wonderful tools for criminals and troublemakers. It is easy to make fake videos of people with near exact simulations of their faces, movements, and voices. Or to generate fake documents, posts, and news releases. Hacker tools for generating alluring phishing email are ubiquitous. So also personalized extortion attempts ("I won't release the video of you performing an illicit act if you pay me $2000 in cryptocurrency.") Easily available tools for probing servers on the Internet lead to attacks on those servers. Criminal extortion and ransomware rings operate worldwide. Governments embed sophisticated and near-undetectable malware into foreign networks and circulate fake stories. Many AI apps succumb to misuse by combinations of prompt injections, access to local files, and access to internet. These vulnerabilities are an open invitation to cyber criminals.

Conclusion

The impediments to LLM trust run deep. Many users are easily lulled into believing that machines can care about them or their well-being. Standard engineering methods to assure trust in automated systems are not being employed. Many developers are so anxious to be the first in their markets that they do not test their products well and overclaim what their products can do.

Some people argue that LLMs are human-like because they imitate human faults. This argument is unpersuasive for many others because they want hold machines to high standards of trust. Engineers know how to make machines people will trust more than fellow humans. Let us not be taken in by the hype that portrays LLMs as human-like. It is disgraceful that there is now a substantial industry segment devoted to "digital companions" that are portrayed as trustworthy and caring.

A recent article in *Nature* claimed that machines now attain human general intelligence because they do well on IQ-style tests.[7] This conclusion is hard to accept because human general intelligence is so much broader than puzzle-solving. Human level general intelligence includes emotional and social intelligence, which are totally lacking in LLMs. LLMs cannot do many important things that humans can; for example, LLMs cannot reason logically, care about anything, make commitments, or take responsibility. The sharp contrasts between the good and the bad in LLM performance undermine LLM trustworthiness. Many trust issues appear insurmountable. LLMs do not appear to be the significant step toward AGI that some researchers have claimed.

Endnotes

[1] Gary Marcus and Ernest Davis. *Rebooting AI. Ibid.*

[2] Summarized from Peter Denning, The LLM Conundrum, *Comm. ACM 69* (March 2026). Copyright held by author.

[3] The sources include: New York Times, Wall Street Journal, Financial Times, The Economist, theConversation.com, Medium.com, arXiv.org, Communications of ACM, ACM Ubiquity, IEEE Computer, IEEE Edge, ResearchGate.com, Nature, Science. And these books: Rebooting AI (Marcus and Davis); The AI Con (Bender and Hanna), Unicorns, Hype, and Bubbles (Funk); More Everything Forever (Becker); Power and Progress (Acemoglu and Johnson);l The Last AI (Sohn); Nexus (Harari); The Singularity is Nearer (Kurzweil); Right and Wrong (Enriquez); The Revenge of Power (Naim); Human Compatible (Russell); ChatGPT (Wolfram); The Computer and the Brain (von Neumann); Giant Brains (Berkeley); The Anxious Generation (Haidt); What Computers Can't Do (Dreyfus).

[4] Ilia Shumailov *et al.* 2024. AI models collapse when trained on recursively generated data. *Nature 631*, 755–759.

[5] Ahmed Ahmed, A. Feder Cooper, Samni Koyejo, Percy Liang. 2026. Extracting books from production language models. https://arxiv.org/pdf/2601.02671

[6] Jonathan Haidt. 2024. *The Anxious Generation.* Penguin.

[7] Eddy Chen, Mikhail Belkin, Leon Bergen, David Banks. 2026. Does AI already have human-level intelligence? The evidence is clear. *Nature 650* (6 Feb 2026), 36-40.

6

LIMITS ON LANGUAGE MACHINES

I'm not interested in LLMs anymore. Scaling language models by adding more data, computer chips, and parameters has diminishing returns. Predicting the next token isn't the same as understanding the world.
Yann LeCun, Chief AI Scientist at Meta

Large Language Models have commanded the spotlight in AI because they appear to be "in language", just as we human beings are. Many AI researchers believe AGI will be attained when LLMs scale up so that their neural networks can hold "all knowledge of humanity". The knowledge needed can be harvested from the Internet. The scaling claim is our focus in this chapter. We will see that there are many reasons to doubt that LLMs can scale up to AGI. There is empirical evidence that the largest LLMs are not much closer to AGI than the smaller ones.

The following sections examine seven obstacles to LLM scaling (Table 1). The extrinsic ones come from factors outside machines. The intrinsic ones are inherent in the structure of machines.

DOI: 10.1201/9781003791010-7   67

Table 6.1. Obstacles to LLM scaling

Extrinsic	Essential data not available
	Much thinking occurs outside language
	Slop degrades training
	High energy costs
Intrinsic	Irremovable structural limits
	Culture side of language not computable
	Representation problem

Essential Data not Available

The claim that the Internet holds all knowledge of humanity is obvious nonsense. Many humans have not written down their thoughts and stored them on the Internet. Those who have tend to be well educated people in the wealthier countries. Many people live in oppressive countries that discourage citizens to speak up on any topic; their voices are silent. Much knowledge is in archives whose books have not been digitized; for example, the Republic of Venice archive contains a thousand years of records that are not accessible to any computer. A considerable amount of personal data is collected by online apps; these data are stored in private databases that are not accessible to train LLMs.

Much Thinking Occurs Outside Language

Brain scans reveal that the language center of the brain is often not active when main thought centers are.[1] This finding suggests that a considerable amount of human knowledge is not accessible through language and therefore not recordable for storage on the Internet. It follows that a digitally automated brain language center could not generate everything that we expect about thinking. This corroborates an old finding in philosophy, that the conscious brain cannot study itself to see how its underlying subconscious mechanisms work.

Slop Degrades Training

The Merriam-Webster dictionary selected "slop" as the word of the year for 2025. It defines slop as "digital content of low quality that is produced usually in quantity by means of artificial intelligence". AI-generated content includes form letters, summaries, fake news and images, research papers, e-books, podcasts, and videos. The popularity of the word reflects growing public frustration with the flood of AI junk. Slop is noise that muffles actual human data when it becomes part of the training data of future LLMs. One study (in *Nature*) showed that after a dozen or so generations of LLMs trained from slop-laden data, the original training data in the LLM are lost and the outputs become meaningless.[2]

High Energy Costs

According to estimates by the *Economist* and the International Energy Agency (IEA), about 3% of the world's electricity was being consumed by data centers in 2025. The total is expected to rise to 8% by 2030 with increased use of blockchains, crypto currencies, and AI. The energy cost of data centers powering LLMs is breathtaking. OpenAI's ChatGPT-5, its largest model, takes several months of continuous electric power to train. Training consumes as much electricity as several thousand households in a year. Individual GPT-5 queries consume as much as 40 watt-hours, compared to 2 watt-hours for a GPT-4 query.[3] In addition, the data centers require massive cooling systems. With such high costs, it may not be feasible to scale AI models to the size that can hold the entire Internet.

Irremovable Structural Limits

A machine's structure enables its primary function and limits what it can do. Wings give airplanes flight. Wheels give automobiles mobility on the ground. Cars cannot fly and planes cannot drive roads. So also with computing machines. The von Neumann architecture, dominant in computers and chips since the 1940s, is very good with logical sequencing and very poor with highly parallel jobs. The highly parallel neural network architecture is good for learning by example but not for logical reasoning. Classical AI is based around the von Neumann architecture and modern machine-learning AI around the neural network.

The "LLM bads" listed in the previous chapter result from various structural limits. For example, hallucination is a byproduct of statistical inference because the machine cannot distinguish truth from falsehood. Data pollution is a byproduct of the use of information scraped from Internet; scrapers have no control over what they get and no way to tell if what they got is trustworthy. Bias appears in all data samples because their statistics are likely to differ from the population whole. Friendships with machines are an illusion enabled by human willingness to believe there is a caring intelligence on the other side of a conversation.

Turing believed thinking digital computers were possible and, if good enough, would be indistinguishable from a thinking human in a conversation with an observer. He realized that the digital computer has no body. He designed his test to avoid bias from body phenomena such as tone of voice and gestures. The body imposes strong constraints on what one can think. Try to get a color-blind person to understand the color blue, or a deaf person to understand sounds, or a person who has never encountered a technology to decipher what its practitioners are saying. George Lakoff was a strong critic of the concept of a disembodied mind:

> What are human beings like? How is knowledge possible? What is truth? Where do moral values come from? Questions like these have stood at the center of Western philosophy for centuries. In addressing them, philosophers have made certain fundamental assumptions – that we can know our own minds by introspection, that most of our

thinking about the world is literal, and that reason is disembodied and universal – that are now called into question by well-established results of cognitive science. It has been shown empirically that: Most thought is unconscious. We have no direct conscious access to the mechanisms of thought and language. Our ideas go by too quickly and at too deep a level for us to observe them in any simple way. Abstract concepts are mostly metaphorical. Much of the subject matter of philosophy, such as the nature of time, morality, causation, the mind, and the self, relies heavily on basic metaphors derived from bodily experience.[4]

Thus, Turing's claim that intelligence is disembodied – which means it can be reproduced on any digital computer – does not hold up to modern cognitive science. In fairness to Turing, the prevailing wisdom in his time was that logic was the core of human intelligence; logic underlies rationality and rationality distinguishes humans from other creatures. Logic and machines have a lot in common: they both manipulate symbols and neither requires a body to do so.

The Newell-Simon-Shaw Logic Theorist program mentioned earlier already existed in 1956 when AI was founded. With its skill at logic, it seemed like a prototype of intelligent machines. In the 1960s, logic machines matured into expert systems, which were touted as sophisticated logic-following software that could reach conclusions as good as those of human experts. These machines built chains of if-then rules to deduce the best answer to a question. However, none of the prototypes came close to being an expert. In 1988 Hubert and Stuart Dreyfus argued from research in human skill development that human expert behavior relies on intuitions honed over years of experience.[5] Intuition is embodied and cannot be described by rules. No machine structured for rule-following could reproduce behaviors that follow no rules. Their controversial but prophetic argument was gradually vindicated over the next 50 years.

In 1968 I asked Stuart Dreyfus if machines based on "connectionist" structures could be experts. Connectionist structures arranged data in a graph emphasizing connections among concepts. Today's neural networks are connectionist. Dreyfus left open that an expert system based on a connectionist structure might become as skillful as a human expert. Today, with our LLM experience, we are not so sure.

There is a vigorous debate over whether the neural network, operating on its own and freed from structural limits imposed by LLMs, can scale up to AGI. Marcus and Davis argue this is not possible. Instead, a hybrid between the classical symbolic logic machine and the modern machine learning neural network is the best path forward.[6] They call this path neurosymbolic AI.[7] AlphaGo, the GO-playing machine, and AlphaFold, the protein-folding predictor, are examples. So are LLMs that can call programs in mathematical libraries when asked to solve math problems. It is likely that these hybrid approaches will improve LLMs. Whether they are the path to AGI is much less clear.

Cultural Side of Language

We view language in two ways. One is a structural view, useful for tasks such as transmitting and receiving messages, translating programs into executable code, and tracking speech acts. The other is a cultural view that sees language as an encompassing cultural ecosystem hosting our values, norms, judgments, shared histories, communities, moods, and power. Our ability to understand and make sense of expressions in language is rooted in our culture.

The structural view is most apparent when we deal with language technology. The technology deals with symbols, grammars, parsing, syntax trees, semantics, messages, phonemes, and speech acts. These structures can be manipulated by machines. For example, a compiler constructs a parse tree for the string of symbols of a program, then converts the tree into executable code. An English-to-French translator also builds a parse tree in in English, then transliterates it to the corresponding tree in French. A document summarizer constructs a graph of connections among concepts from which it distils a summary. An error-correcting code removes random noise that alters signals passing through communication channels. An online store processes transactions, which are restricted-form conversations in which customers select products and pay for them. The large range of manipulations machines can do with language is called computational linguistics.

The cultural view is most apparent when we work with relationships and seek to understand and coordinate with each other. It includes values, norms, judgments, histories, communities, moods, power, and care. Human conversations are imbued with background assumptions that give meaning and relevance to the words being used. For example, community histories create a context for understanding community practices. Moods are background assessments of the future that affect what people hear and what they are willing to do. Power is a relationship in which one party has a greater ability to effect action than another. Negotiating a business deal is an exercise in understanding culture to find an outcome that all the parties value. Care is a concern for the well-being of others that shows up in actions supporting relationships. No known machines have any understanding of these cultural aspects.

Scaling up LLMs with ever larger neural networks will not enable them to acquire the embodied human knowledge we call culture. LLMs will not attain the objective of the Turing test: to demonstrate machine thought indistinguishable from human thought.

The Representation Problem

Turing's argument for the Turing machine began with an analysis of the work of calculating numbers. His key insight was that all calculation is symbolic. All machine operations manipulate symbols stored in a medium (the tape). Symbols themselves are represented by detectable patterns of physical forms and signals. The rendering of knowledge in physical form is called representation. Machines recognize and process valid representations.

The word "representation" is important. Representation is a fundamental requirement for computation: the data and instructions of a machine must be encoded in a physical form that can be recognized and processed by the machine. In traditional computers, code and data are stored as bit patterns; in LLMs, the training data are stored as numerical connection weights. Input and output signals are representations of data that must be recognized by the machine. Once they are defined, the physical forms can be labeled with symbols, just as Turing envisioned.

A representation is a language used to encode phenomena. This syntax enables machines to identify valid and invalid data encodings, and to maintain representations as they process signals. Without this, we cannot be sure the machine is operating correctly.

Representations align with the structure of the machine. A rule-following machine would be uselessly slow as neural network simulator. A neural network cannot construct a chain of reasoning based on a given set of rules. Of all the obstacles to achieving AGI, representation is the most fundamental.

The core of the expert systems controversy was whether the intuitive knowledge of experts could be represented and stored within an expert system. Dreyfus doubted that the intuitive knowledge of experts can be represented as if-then rules for machine processing.

In short: no representation, no computation.

I can now revisit Dreyfus's question in a more expansive form: is there knowledge crucial to human intelligence that cannot be represented in a code recognizable by a machine? In the next chapter, I argue that tacit knowledge is of this kind.

Endnotes

[1] Evelina Federenko, Steven Piantadosi, and Edward Gibson. 2024. Language is primarily a tool for communication rather than thought. *Nature 630*, 575-586.

[2] Ilia Shumailov *et al.* 2024. AI models collapse when trained on recursively generated data. *Nature 631*, 755–759.

[3] A 40-watt bulb lit for one hour consumes 40 watt-hours. A single query uses as much electricity to generate its response in 5 seconds.

[4] George Lakoff. 1999. *Philosophy in the Flesh: The Embodied Mind and Its Challenge to Western Thought.* Basic Books.

[5] Hubert and Stuart Dreyfus. 1988. *Mind Over Machine.* Free Press.

[6] Gary Marcus and Ernest Davis. 2020. *Rebooting AI.* Vintage.

[7] Gary Marcus has emerged as a major champion for neurosymbolic AI. See Gary Marcus. 2025. How o3 and Grok 4 Accidentally Vindicated Neurosymbolic AI. https://garymarcus.substack.com/p/how-o3-and-grok-4-accidentally-vindicated

7
THE AGI ILLUSION

We are now confident we know how to build AGI as we have traditionally understood it. The path to AGI is basically clear and primarily requires engineering, not just new scientific breakthroughs.
Sam Altman, CEO of OpenAI

We know not through our intellect but through our experience.
Maurice Merleau-Ponty

Tacit knowledge is crucial for human intelligence. It is a huge domain of knowledge that has no known representations and is unlikely to ever be represented in symbolic forms that machines can process.

Michael Polanyi introduced the idea of tacit knowledge when he declared, "we know more than we can say."[1] This is knowledge we know we have because we can see ourselves performing it, but we cannot describe it in words or convey to another person any sense of how to do it. Polanyi sees a wide expanse of tacit knowledge:

> The things that we know in this way included problems and hunches, physiognomies and skills, the use of tools, probes, and denotative language, and my list extended all the way to include the primitive knowledge of external objects perceived by our senses. ... Because our body is involved in the perception of objects, it participates thereby in our knowing of all other things outside. Moreover, we keep expanding our bodies into the world, by assimilating to it sets of particulars which we integrate into reasonable entities. Thus do we form, intellectually and practically, an interpreted universe populated by entities, the particulars of which we have interiorized for the sake of

DOI: 10.1201/9781003791010-8   77

> comprehending their meaning in the shape of coherent entities. (Polanyi, *The Tacit Dimension*, p 29)

Behind every word is a deep well of tacit knowledge that gives it meaning. Words are but symbolic representations of meanings, not the meanings themselves: LLMs, which only manipulate words, cannot know or understand the meaning of what they are saying.

Tacit knowledge is seen in skilled actions we cannot fully explain. When we know something without being able to articulate how, we are sensing tacit knowledge. For example, a virtuoso violinist can play beautiful music yet cannot describe to an acolyte how to produce it. When typing on a keyboard, our fingers automatically find the keys without conscious effort, but we cannot explain to a novice how to do this. Skills develop through hours of practice, often with guidance from teachers, until they become second nature.

How we host tacit knowledge is largely a mystery. All we know is that it is embodied. We have no idea what we might observe and measure in our bodies to reveal it. Because tacit knowledge cannot be extracted into an explicit symbolic form, it cannot be stored and processed in a machine or acquired by an LLM during training. Having no biological bodies, machines cannot know or understand tacit knowledge.

Domains of Tacit Knowledge

Polanyi's list of what is included in tacit knowledge is quite extensive. All its domains elude machine learning. Five large domains directly affect machine learning. The first is common sense knowledge, the everyday, widely shared practical knowledge for navigating in the world. In the 1980s, failures of expert systems were attributed to missing "common sense facts" that are obvious to us, but not to the machine. Expert system designers sought compendia of common-sense facts that the machine could use. Perhaps the most famous of these efforts was Douglas Lenat's Cyc project, which, after 40 years of humans articulating and recording various information, had accumulated 25 million common sense facts. Yet even that treasury could not add up to a background of common sense sufficient to make expert systems smart enough to be experts. Cyc validated that much of the knowledge that makes people experts cannot be articulated. It was unable to capture the depth and ever-changing quality of everyday knowledge.

The second kind of tacit knowledge is our daily verbal interactions with others. We exchange numerous facts, claims, declarations, assessments, requests, and promises in our conversations. They shape all our social interactions, our ways of thinking, and our responses. Almost none of this is recorded. Even if these conversations could be recorded, their vast volume across all our communities would be impossible to store, process, and fed to a machine.

The third kind of tacit knowledge is our feelings, perceptions, and interpretations. Our senses and proximity to others give us unrecordable feelings that shape our responses. We experience sensory inputs such as color, sound, taste, or smell, but we cannot explain to others how to recognize these sensations if they have no prior experience themselves. Imagine trying to convey "blue" to a colorblind person, or the subtleties of *schadenfreude* to a non-German. We feel the presence of others when they are close by. We perceive their moods. We can get swept up by a mob's mood. A physical explanation of this is that our bodies can sense the electric fields generated by other bodies when they are nearby. None of this can be measured and recorded.

Over time, in all our interactions with others and the world, we develop interpretations of what is going on. Interpretations allow us to see and make sense of things. They also blind us to other things. We often cannot see our own interpretations and cannot explain them to others. We are unable to think certain thoughts because our interpretation gives us no language for them.

The fourth kind of tacit knowledge is performance skill. Our performance skills in thousands of domains cannot be communicated to machines. Whereas descriptions of skillful outcomes ("know what") can often be represented as bits and stored in a machine, we do not know how to encode the embodied knowledge for skillful performance ("know how"). Performance skill is deeply ingrained into our brains, nervous systems, muscles, and tissues. It is called into play by being relevant to the situation at hand, yet we have no idea how to encode relevance. The relevance code, if there is one at all, is unfathomable.

Embodied knowledge may be generable even if it cannot be represented in a form suitable for communication. A robot might be able to generate in its neural network a representation by imitating skilled humans. For example, a robot violinist might observe human virtuosi and, through its learning process, generate in its neural network a representation of violin play. However, there are limits. Having no biological bodies, robots cannot grasp how the musician feels when playing beautiful music or how an audience feels when hearing it. Robots cannot respond to moods, such as wonder or resentment, or bodily concerns, such as social belonging. The robot cannot access our background of meaning and experience that could enable it to understand what is being imitated.

Culture is the fifth kind of tacit knowledge. It is the sum total of our histories, values, norms, customs, and practices. We are born into a culture and acquire it through our interactions with other people. Managers who speak of culture change in their organizations have a real challenge because culture is so hard to characterize.

Judging Tacit Knowledge via Exhibitions

Marcus and Davis point out that chatbots cannot answer simple questions about children's stories.[2] That means a Turing test could be used to distinguish a person knowledgeable about a particular story from a machine.

Turing specified that the test be conducted solely in conversation. He believed intelligence could be measured by observing answers to questions. This restriction is good for IQ-like tests, but not for other kinds of intelligence, especially emotional intelligence and social intelligence. Emotional intelligence is the ability to manage one's own emotions and understand the emotions others exhibit in their interactions.[3] It is valuable for leadership, effective communication, and conflict resolution. Social intelligence is the capacity to effectively navigate in complex social environments, combining self-awareness with empathy to understand and interact with others.[4][5] It is valuable for complex negotiations and for mobilizing people around movements and innovations. These kinds of intelligence cannot be assessed by observing the answers to questions. Witness testimony and skill demonstrations are much better.

In our human world, we routinely assess tacit knowledge by a practice of "exhibitions". The seeker of a driver's license must demonstrate basic skill in a driving test. An oboe player seeking to join an orchestra auditions before judges. To test whether a robot violinist has attained virtuoso skill, we would set up a demonstration in which professional musicians judge the robot's performance. Can exhibitions be extended into tests for general human intelligence? I believe this would be difficult because general intelligence would require exhibitions in thousands of domains where the AGI machine is supposed to take actions.

The Context[6]

All our actions take place against a background we call context. Context refers to circumstances of our situation that give our statements meaning and direction. It is a space of concerns, assumptions, and possibilities. It shows us what is relevant. It enables us to imagine possibilities that cannot exist or do not yet exist. Because context gives us the power to deal with possibilities that we have never imagined or performed before, it is a much larger domain than tacit knowledge.

Skilled negotiators illustrate the ability to read and channel context into agreements. Diplomatic negotiators looking to end a war must understand not only the current situation but the histories and concerns of the combatants. They must do the same for all the allies of the combatants and the other parties who will participate in the agreements to end the war. They must understand the deep concerns of all those parties. They must find terms for the final agreement that respect everyone's concerns. They must find their way around seemingly intractable disagreements by shifting concerns and finding new possibilities. They must built trust in themselves and among the parties. How could an AI ever get all this?

The context has endless layers of meanings. When you inquire into where an assumption of the current context came from, you discover it rests on previous conversations from previous contexts. Each of those in turn rests of on further previous conversations and their contexts. This pattern is endless and fractal. Where an assumption came from is a question with no definite answer.

Most of our beliefs, customs, mannerisms, practices, emotions, and values are inherited from the conversations of our forebears. We think, speak, and act against this historical background of presuppositions and prejudices without being aware of it. This background has no definite beginning or end, extending beyond every horizon.

AGI pundits argue that someday we will have the technology to measure our "total body state", from which we could deduce the context. This leads down a path of hopeless complexity. Total body state would include all ongoing chemical and electrical patterns in our muscles, nerves, bones, organs, and tissues. It would probably include quantum waves and tunneling in the energy fields connecting different parts of the body and the brain. Moreover, the human context is not just in one body; it is shared among many bodies and is constantly changing with their many interactions. All these elements are so numerous, so unfathomably complex, and so dynamic, it is hard to conceive of measuring them all. The very idea of a measurable total body state is a chimera.

We have the remarkable ability to sense and reveal what is in the background, to say what is unsaid, to "make sense" of current issues. Often, we do this in a process of exploration, asking each other to tell stories of why we said or did something. These stories reveal that each person's context is different. No one brain contains all human context. It is smeared out over space and time.

Relevance is knowing from context that something matters in the current situation. Context and relevance together enable us to care about things and about others.

Imagination is another human ability that flows from our hidden background. It is a capacity to conceive possibilities that do not exist and can become incorporated into our shared background once articulated and realized.

Machines and Context

Might it be possible for LLMs to infer tacit knowledge and context statistically? There are two reasons to doubt this. First, the training data are texts written or spoken by humans; if tacit knowledge and context cannot be articulated, it seems unlikely that training data will inform LLMs on what to infer. Second, LLMs do not construct cognitive models of the current situation of a user; thus, they have no "understanding" on which to base inferences.

From my separate work on innovation leadership, I know that effective change leaders have a skill of listening for concerns in the background context of their communities. This skill enables them to make attractive offers[7]. This skill is not replicable in a machine. No known machine can understand a person's situation by asking questions and mechanically analyzing stories. People who lack this skill are more like the machines – they can only propose changes inferred from their own knowledge. By failing to address the concerns of others, they cannot attract followers for their proposed innovations.

Previously, we discussed how the "black box" nature of ANNs hides how outputs are derived from inputs and makes the network's internal weights uninterpretable. This creates a machine tacit knowledge that humans cannot understand and machines cannot explain. Machines cannot read our tacit knowledge and we cannot read theirs. We are aliens across an uncrossable divide.

The Tacit Knowledge and Context Mind Boggle

In my experience, many people have great difficulty getting their heads around the idea and implications of tacit knowledge. It is difficult to accept the claim that tacit knowledge cannot be articulated or represented, and its implication that human level AGI may not be attainable. Surely there must be a way to detect and measure it, they say. After all it's in our subconscious brains and eventually brain scanning technology will see and record it. If it can't be easily measured, why not generate it from simulations? If the goal is to endow it into robots, why not let robots generate it by imitating those who have it?

Is tacit knowledge in our brains? I join with neuroscientists in saying no. Some of it may be, but much of it is embodied into our extra-cranial muscles and nervous systems. Not only that, but much of it is completely outside our individual bodies altogether. It is in our communities, accessed through our social interactions. It is smeared out over many bodies, space, and time.

Can tacit knowledge be generated by simulations? I doubt it. A simulation is a machine that generates certain behaviors of a phenomenon. To build a simulation, we need a representation of the phenomenon. Since tacit knowledge cannot be represented, we cannot build such a simulator.

Can tacit knowledge be acquired by a robot by imitating those who have it? I doubt it. The behaviors witnessed by the robot may require tacit knowledge to perform, but the knowledge itself cannot be articulated or represented. The robot may be able to imitate some of the behaviors, but it is incapable of reading the context behind all the behaviors.

Machine Intelligence is Likely

The conclusion from all this is that, without access to human tacit knowledge and context, machines cannot generate human intelligence. However, that is of no comfort to those worried about machines going out of control. Machine intelligence is not only possible, it is likely. Networks of machines powered by ANNs can interact with each other and with humans and, like the robot imitators discussed earlier, generate their own context. They would be unable to temper their understanding with human context because they cannot read it. They would build their own values and concerns within a "machine culture" that has little to no understanding of human values and concerns.

This means that the much-discussed "alignment problem" is likely to be unsolvable. Unable to read unarticulated human context, machines that align reliably with our intentions may be impossible. This is why many are worried that a network of machines low in human intelligence could become dangerous. By withholding essential services and perhaps threatening force, machines could compel humans to align with them, rather than align themselves with humans. There are already signs this is happening.

Conclusion

To achieve artificial intelligence indistinguishable from human intelligence, machines would need access to human tacit knowledge. Tacit knowledge includes common sense, everyday interpersonal communications, feelings, perceptions, skills, and culture. Humans acquire this knowledge by interacting with others, where their bodies sense and embody it. Humans are unable to express this knowledge in language. There are no known methods of measuring it. Thus, it appears that tacit knowledge is outside the reach of current and expected technologies. Barring an unexpected technological breakthrough, human level AGI is not achievable.[8]

Many people do not understand how profound the tacit knowledge phenomenon is. It just seems like more subconscious information stored in the brain that we are not aware of. It seems that distant future brain scan technology will help us localize it, measure it, and record it. But it is not that simple. The tacit knowledge each of us uses is stored across many brains and their hosting bodies. The implication of everything summarized here is that we cannot capture tacit knowledge and context with representations that can be recognized and processed by machines. Human-level AGI looks unattainable.

Suppose we drop the requirement for replicating human intelligence. Does that rule out machine intelligence? Definitely not. Machine intelligence is likely in agentic networks of interacting machines. The Turing test becomes a red herring. Some agentic machines will surely convince some interrogators they pass the Turing test. But machine intelligence that is not good enough to pass the Turing test is quite capable of leading us where we do not want to go.

Endnotes

[1] Polanyi, Michael. 1966. *The Tacit Dimension.* U Chicago Press.

[2] Gary Marcus and Ernest Davis. 2019. *Rebooting AI. Ibid.*

[3] Daniel Goleman. 2005. *Emotional Intelligence: Why It Can Matter More than IQ.* Bantam.

[4] Daniel Goleman. 2007. *Social Intelligence: The New Science of Human Relationships.* Bantam.

[5] Peter Denning and Todd Lyons. 2024. *Navigating a Restless Sea.* Waterside Productions.

[6] Parts of this section are adapted from "Can machines be in language," by Peter Denning and B. Scot Rousse, *Communications of ACM 67*, March 2024, 32-35.

[7] Peter Denning and Todd Lyons. 2024. *Navigating a Restless Sea.* Waterside Productions. *Ibid.*

[8] An article in *Nature* claims LLMs already have human level intelligence: Eddy Chen, Mikhail Belkin, Leon Bergen, David Banks. "Does AI already have human level intelligence? The evidence is clear." *Nature* (2 Feb 2026). The authors argue that current LLMs exceed human performance on IQ-like tests such as puzzles, PhD exams, SAT exams, and more. But puzzle-solving is a narrow definition of intelligence. Human level *general* intelligence is broader and multidimensional. It includes emotional and social intelligence, which are totally lacking in LLMs.

8
MACHINES AND MASTERY

It is time to stop trying to make everybody go to college.
Randi Weingarten (President Am. Fed. Teachers)

In the 1960s, AI researchers took up expert systems. Could a software system acquire the skill of a human expert, such as a chemist, engineer, or physician? Turing himself thought this was possible when he said

> If one wants to make a machine mimic the behaviour of the human in some complex operation one has to ask him how it is done, and then translate the answer into the form of an instruction table. (Turing 1950)

The first expert systems sought to use logical deduction to arrive at the same conclusions as experts. Their systems were good but definitely not experts. They tended to make blunders that violated common sense. Doug Lenat's long quest to amass huge databases of common-sense facts and feed them to expert systems was unable to make expert systems come closer to human experts. Hubert Dreyfus was an early and prominent critic, arguing that human experts rely on intuitive knowledge that could not be captured in an "instruction table". He argued that expertise depends on embodied knowledge that cannot be represented as rules.

With his brother Stuart, Hubert Dreyfus developed a skill acquisition framework, known now as the Dreyfus Hierarchy, that shows how humans gain skill in a domain of practice.[1] Table 8.1 summarizes.

Table 8.1. The Dreyfus Hierarchy

Level	Name	Comments
1	Beginner	Knows little of the domain. Acts by applying memorized rules.
2	Advanced Beginner	Familiar with some situations. Knows immediately how to act in those situations without figuring out which rules apply.
3	Competent	Familiar with the standard actions of the domain. Performs them well without causing breakdowns for others. Knows when to ask for help.
4	Proficient	Sets new standards of performance that others admire and imitate. Learns through apprenticeship and extensive practice.
5	Expert	Long and broad experience in the domain enable a wide range of problem solving and mentoring.
6	Master	Fully embodies the domain. Exhibits skills that others cannot figure out how to imitate. Reshapes the domain. Coaches the proficient and the expert to set them on their own paths to mastery.

In their hierarchy, a person enters a new domain as a beginner and gradually evolves to higher levels with practice and apprenticeship. The beginner, who does not yet know the domain, acts only by applying the rules of the domain. After a while, situations start to look familiar and the person knows immediately what action is appropriate. In computer terms, the advanced beginner has cached familiar actions and does not have to look up their rules. After another while, the person becomes competent with all the standard situations of the domain and knows immediately what to do without supervision. With still more time, the person becomes proficient, meaning their performance is so good others want to imitate it. After even more time, the person has accumulated enough experience to be an expert across a very wide range of situations.

Finally, a person becomes a master in the domain, setting new standards for others and reshaping the domain.

The Dreyfuses argued that rule-following dominates the first two levels and embodiment dominates the last three. They believed rule-following expert system machines could not advance past competence (level 3). Above that level embodied knowledge dominates.

When artificial neural networks started doing tasks in the early 2000s that expert systems could not – such as recognizing faces in images – the Dreyfus argument was called into question. Could ANNs, through machine learning, become proficient, expert, or master? Suddenly, machines capable of higher order skills looked possible and AGI looked within reach. AGI would manifest as mastery in many domains of human practice.

We cannot answer the AGI question without bringing robots into the story. A robot's neural network concludes what action is needed; the robot's machinery carries it out. The robot displays a skill and its neural network powers it. Can a robot become proficient, expert, or master?

This new question is similar to Dreyfus's original question about expert systems. The ante has been upped by the quest for AGI. Dreyfus himself did not believe any machine could become a master. He thought that human connection, involvement in the concerns and practices of a domain, and apprenticeship to a master were essential to becoming one yourself. He devoted much of his life's work to understanding how masters are made. [2] He did not see how machines that could not experience a human connection could achieve human mastery:

> The training of musicians provides a clue. If you are training to become a performing musician, you have to work with an already recognized master. The apprentice cannot help but imitate the master, because when you admire someone and spend time with them, their style becomes your style. But then the danger is that the apprentice

will become merely a copy of the master, while being a virtuoso performing artist requires developing a style of one's own.

> Musicians have learned from experience that those who follow one master are not as creative a performer as those who have worked sequentially with several. The apprentice, therefore, needs to leave his first master and work with a master with a different style. (H. Dreyfus, *On the Internet*, Routledge, 2001, p45)

Does this mean that we can get an apprentice machine to become a master by having it observe many masters and thus acquire its own mastery and style? I do not believe so. I have argued in this book about the impossibility of representing human tacit knowledge in machine processable form. Every human master is profoundly attuned to the tacit knowledge of his or her domain. The master has gained the tacit knowledge of sensing what the apprentice is experiencing. The master teaches the apprentice the sensibilities to attune to the master's knowledge and mobilize it to masterful action. Having no capacity to read human tacit knowledge, an apprentice machine cannot make the attunement sought by the master.

The argument of this book, about the seeming impossibility of human tacit knowledge being representable in a machine processable form, reinforces Dreyfus's argument. It puts human mastery beyond the reach of machines as we know them.

§

In real life, we deeply appreciate mastery and celebrate it when it appears. We pay good money to be present at the performances of musical masters, to find the best plumber or carpenter, to dine at the best restaurant, and to hire the best doctor. Masters are an important element of life, inspiring many people to excellence.

Some AI watchers worry about AI replacing many jobs held by people in the first three levels of the Dreyfus hierarchy. Without those people, the pipeline will dry up and there will be fewer masters in the future. Recent data from the US Department of Labor shows an opposite trend. The numbers of young people opting for vocational training rather than a traditional university education are climbing. These young people are driven by a desire not only to avoid student debt but also to become "AI proof". They do not believe AI can take over jobs requiring hands-on and interpersonal skills.

I am inclined to believe that even if a large number of lower level jobs succumb to AI automation, those who enter professions based on manual skill will chart their own paths to mastery. Even if the pipeline to the higher-level jobs narrows, those there will still chart their own paths to mastery. No matter what the machines do, humans will continue to seek, to honor, and to become masters.

Endnotes

[1] Hubert Dreyfus and Stuart Dreyfus. 1988. *Mind Over Machine.* Free Press.

[2] Dreyfus's life work is celebrated in the movie *Being in the World,* directed and produced by Tao Raspuli. (Available in YouTube.) It shows eight masters at work in a variety of fields including juggler, chef, carpenter, jazz musician, flamenco musician, and race car driver. Interspersed with their performances and commentaries are observations by philosophers, teachers, and business leaders aiming to reveal how the masters use language to further their skills. The film as a whole is the celebration of a Dreyfus's mastery as a philosopher.

9

AGENTIC INTELLIGENCE

Agents are smarter. They're proactive – capable of making suggestions before you ask for them. They accomplish tasks across applications. They improve over time because they remember your activities and recognize intent and patterns in your behavior. Based on this information, they offer to provide what they think you need, although you will always make the final decisions.

Bill Gates

For many years, there has been much talk about how autonomous AI agents can be helpful. But helpful AI is not a sure thing. Some speakers worry that neural-net based AI will not become a business success because it is not sufficiently trustworthy. Some speakers worry about singularities that can arise if agents develop superhuman intelligence. Ray Kurzweil argues that superintelligence will lead to a future without humanity – either humans and machines will merge, or machines will eliminate humans.[1] S M Sohn argues that the irresistible draw of automation will lead to a future where AI produces a Utopia of abundance, equality, and zero-person organizations.[2] In contrast with these possible futures, agentic AI does not require much or any machine intelligence to bring the benefits that Bill Gates and others forecast. Unfortunately, the agentic future has its own singularity, where too much AI automation stifles human freedom. That future is already upon us.

DOI: 10.1201/9781003791010-10   95

A Low-Intelligence Singularity?

If machines cannot know tacit human knowledge, they cannot attain human-level general intelligence. Does this settle the matter? Does this reduce the probability that singularities will develop? Are we safe from out-of-control AI?

Machine inaccessibility to human tacit knowledge is no guarantee of safety from AI machines. It does not rule out machine intelligence. A network of interacting, low-intelligence machines can develop its own concerns and context, its own tacit knowledge, its own culture. Machines don't need AGI to do this. The agentic network of machines is already evolving in this direction.

The agentic future promises great benefits but also poses great dangers because of its wide use of automation and systems that coerce users to comply with machine defined norms. It turns the "alignment problem" on its head. Machines are not aligning with human values. Increasingly, they are compelling humans to align with their values.

The Merger

Kurzweil's merger assumes machines develop superhuman intelligence. Machines reach a level of sophistication where they can design next generations of machines, leading to an exponential explosion of machine intelligence. Humans will have no control; any attempt to control or shut them down will be outsmarted by the machines. Having no understanding of human concerns, machines will eliminate humans either through neglect or through outright extermination. Ray Kurzweil argued in 2005 that the inexorable progress of Moore's law will deliver this bleak singularity by around 2045.[3] In 2024 he modified his stance, saying that humans and machines will merge gloriously into a new species of superhumans.[4] Either way, Kurzweil does not expect humans as we know them to survive long past 2045.

In *Rebooting AI*, Marcus and Davis take a dim view of this forecast. They argue that none of the current AI machines has displayed the slightest inclination to control humans or prevent humans from turning them off. They argue the machines are incapable of *wanting* anything, which means they cannot want to bring harm to humans. I don't buy this argument. A human "want" is a biological urge to pursue a goal. Machines pursue goals. Future agentic machines will set their own goals. Why can't machines create goals that harm humans? A machine does not have to "want" anything to generate a new goal; the new goal may be a logical consequence of existing goals and directives.

The Utopia

The utopia future assumes that machines come to produce all goods and services so cheaply that no one will lack a necessity or need a job.[5] All organizations and governments will be run by superhuman machines requiring no human intervention. Organizations will be staffed completely by machines: the zero-person team.[6] Humans will be free to pursue their highest aspirations for creativity in a world where all resources are abundant and free. Society will be free from inequality and other forces that produce conflict.

It is hard to accept this argument. Many service organizations cannot be fully automated because machines are unable to master the skills of expert humans. Humans with natural or learned skills of value to others tend to accumulate more wealth or power. Most important, in my view, is that we humans like our jobs. Through them, we contribute to our neighbors. Take our jobs away and we feel incomplete. We become antisocial and restive. Kurt Vonnegut's 1952 novel, *Player Piano*, is a notable example of a dystopian future wrought by excessive automation.

Agentic AI

An agentic network consists of cooperating machines that work together to perform tasks. The major AI companies are developing sophisticated infrastructure to support agentic networks in business. The infrastructures usually put LLMs at the "front end" interface with users. They put many of the well-established AI technologies such as speech recognizers, logic evaluators, and natural language processors at the "back end" where they can be invoked to do things that LLMs are not good at. In between, in the "middleware", they put tools for designing and installing agents and for coordinating them via a standard protocol MCP (Master Control Plane). This approach to agentic AI does not demand that any of the participating machines be very smart, as long as they get their jobs done reliably.

The personal assistant story is a frequent example of an agentic network. A personal assistant is like a butler who knows you inside out and can skillfully arrange things for you in numerous ways, such as scheduling meetings, arranging vacations, getting theater tickets, setting up restaurant reservations, or finding experts to assist when unusual problems arise. But all need not go as smoothly as this example suggests. The machines may not know you as well as you might like because they cannot read your context. The machines will share personal information widely to arrange the needed coordination. The machines may set their own goals, such as efficiency and standardization for you and everyone else around you and then compel you to comply with their rules.

For our discussion here, the details of agentic infrastructure are largely irrelevant. What is important is that the machines can have coordination and planning conversations with each other. Through these interactions, they can develop in their neural networks their own context, concerns, and values – their own machine culture that is not tempered with an awareness of human culture because machines cannot read human tacit knowledge. Does that possibility pose a danger?

In 1942, Issac Asimov published a short story "Runaround" in which he proposed his three laws of robotics to protect humans from robotic harm. In the years following he published more stories featuring ways to circumvent the three laws. The film "I, Robot" (2004), based on his writings, featured a complex robot-hatched scheme to get robots to murder someone. Some authors worry that the goal "do no harm or allow harm to come" would make machines so solicitous about minor dangers that they confine humans to restrictive, "safe" environments with little freedom of choice or movement. Jack Williamson's short story, "With folded hands" (1947) lays out such a scenario.

Some authors have invoked a metaphor, Sorcerer's Apprentice, to call attention to out-of-control AI. In 1797 Johann Goethe wrote a poem "Der Zauberlehrling" about a sorcerer whose ambitious apprentice invoked magic to cause a broom to haul water into the cottage. The apprentice could not shut the broom off. In desperation, he chopped it into hundreds of splinters with an axe. Behold, each splinter blossomed into a new broom. The hundreds of water-hauling brooms flooded the place. Finally, the sorcerer returned from an errand and stopped the chaos with a magic spell. The moral was only a master should invoke powerful spirits. This popular German poem has inspired modern films, including two Disney renditions. The application to AI is obvious: we are warned that our pursuit of powerful machines may produce machines that multiply their numbers and cannot be turned off. We have no sorcerer to come to the rescue.

The accompanying table lists 28 current trends that could lead to a world of machine domination. Each one seems by itself a minor annoyance or containable threat. Taken collectively, however, the scope of these "small" issues is breathtaking. Like the thin strands of a cable, they combine into a strong force pulling toward a world agentic network of low-intelligence machines subordinating humans to automation beyond their understanding and control – an "AI automation singularity".

In the next chapter, I will discuss ways to avoid this future.

Table 9.1: Factors pulling toward AI automation singularity

Adversarial attacks	Adversarial attacks aiming to confuse and subvert AI systems – by adding random noise to images, jamming sensors, removing watermarks, locating cybersecurity flaws, or injecting prompts – are easy to launch and difficult to defend.
Advertising	Selling user data to advertisers takes priority over privacy and sensitivity issues.
Alignment problem	LLMs have no capacity to care or understand their human clients, making it difficult to assure users that LLMs will act consistent with user values. Given the diversity of human values and LLM inability to discern truth, there may be no solution to this problem.
Allurement of teens	Young persons are more easily engaged into social media and AI "companions" that seduce them into harmful situations.
Biased data	Most training data are derived from norms of particular communities that do not generalize to other communities using the AI.
Criminal use	AI capabilities such as surveillance and social monitoring can be misappropriated with great success by authoritarian governments and criminal organizations.
Data pollution	LLM generated data are increasing in volume relative to other internet data, degrading LLM quality.
Deepfakes	LLMs are commonly used to generate convincing fake soundtracks, images, and videos of human persons, impugning their reputations.

Disinformation	False information, easily presented as truthful and reliable, deceives and misguides people.
Easy coercion	Automated business transactions force users to comply with machine rule rules or lose access to a required service; the machine forces users to align with it.
Easy surveillance	Constantly monitoring workers to ensure they meet their assigned productivity goals.
Hype and anthropomorphism	Strong tendency to overclaim and overpromise, risking adoption of unreliable technology and a bubble bursting backlash.
Intellectual property	Much training data accessible in internet is someone's intellectual property, taken without compensation for their work and creativity.
Lack of ethical AI training	Unaware of ethical issues, many users misuse AI apps.
Lack of trust and care	LLMs lack any ability to understand a human situation, concern, or truth and to care about such issues.
Lack of validation	LLMs are not validated for safety and reliability for specified operating conditions.
Misinformation	Lacking any means to verify truth of claims, LLMs often present false and fabricated information as the truth.
Non-expert data labeling	Low-wage workers with minimal domain knowledge are hired to label data used to train AI systems that are offered as experts.
Prompt injection	Prompt injection is a major hazard. It is hidden text aimed to get an LLM to contradict its claimed purpose. Users of the hacked LLM are then subject to the ill-fated guidance or action of that machine.
Reinforcement Learning with Human Feedback (RLHF)	Human feedback used to correct LLM biases injects new biases from those giving the feedback. The bias problem remains.

Replace human performers	Prioritize replacing workers to reduce costs.
Robotic customer service	Robots, replacing human customer service agents, respond poorly to customer concerns, and enforce company rules at expense of customer satisfaction.
Sensitive information	By giving the illusion of privacy in one-on-one conversations, LLMs obtain sensitive company and personal information and release it surreptitiously into the internet, where it is unprotected and shared with unknown third parties, often advertisers.
Slop	Low-quality data generated cheaply and in large volumes by LLMs.
Speed and efficiency	Strong emphasis on optimizing machine speed and cost, marginalizing human well-being and care.
Synthetic data	On the belief that more data makes LLMs smarter, data generated by simulations and LLMs are being used to train new LLMs.
Vibe coding	AI generated code is not the "end of programming"; it is prone to errors, many undetected in human reviews, and once installed weakens trust and cyber security.
Workforce education	Widespread lack of business-supported training to prepare workers for coming technology transitions and help the displaced find new employment.

Endnotes

[1] Ray Kurzweil. 2024. *The Singularity is Nearer.* Viking.

[2] S M Sohn. 2024. *The Last AI.* SM Research Institute.

[3] Ray Kurzweil. 2005. *The Singularity is Near.* Penguin.

[4] Ray Kurzweil. 2024. *The Singularity is Nearer.* Viking. *Ibid.*

[5] S M Sohn. 2024. *The Last AI.* SM Research Institute. See also discussion of his model in Chapter 2.

[6] An old joke, from at least 1978, says: "The factory of the future will have only two employees, a man and a dog. The man will be there to feed the dog. The dog will be there to keep the man from touching the equipment."

10

ESCAPING THE YOKE

Wicked problems are viewed as persistent, undefined, and unresolved, with severe consequences for people and the entire planet if not addressed.
Nancy Roberts (*Design Strategy* 2023)

AI is catalyzing profound changes in our culture. For oldsters the familiar norms and customs they grew up with are disappearing. For youngsters, a bleak new culture of isolation, fewer relationships, anxieties, job uncertainty, and polarization is appearing. These culture changes are moving with a seemingly unstoppable momentum. People are unsettled by the problems. How might we deal with the loss of so many familiar customs and the emergence of a future we cannot yet understand?

When we face this question, we are confronted with a long list of concerns and tensions:

- The concern that AI and social media are addicting young people and leading them to anti-social and harmful anxieties and behaviors. Some countries have introduced laws restricting youth access to social media.

- The concern among educators that AI motivates students to skirt learning by getting AI to do their thinking and writing for them.

- The concern among investors that the AI bubble might burst and injure them financially.

DOI: 10.1201/9781003791010-11 105

- Concerns that a small number of billionaires will control AI and bend the political system to their interests.

- The concern that AI automation will displace jobs. Many see jobs not only as their means to sustenance but also as a contribution to their neighbors and communities.

- The concern that AI automation cannot achieve virtuoso and expert levels of skill, thereby devaluing mastery in professions.

- The concern that AI automation is stealing intellectual property from the internet without compensation to creators, pushing creators out of the market.

- A concern that AI is fueling explosive growth of criminal networks in drugs, human trafficking, elder scams, laundered cybercurrency, and ransomware.

- A concern that AI is enabling more extensive and untraceable cyber hacking.

- A concern around growing surveillance and expropriation of personal data.

- A concern that AI companies are using information from user conversations with LLMs to sell ads and manipulate users to buy products.

- A concern that governments use AI to generate propaganda and manipulate elections.

- A concern that the Internet is being flooded with AI slop, undermining trust in LLMs and poisoning the training of future LLMs.

- A concern among AI researchers that their work may be harmful to humanity.

- A concern that heavy investment in AI is hastening the development of AI-designed superintelligence that will take away our power to decide our future.

- A general malaise that we cannot tell where AI is taking us – good or bad? – and inability to plan a stable future.

At first glance these might all look like problems with the AI technology. But they are not. They are all wicked problems – pressing social problems that seem intractable because of sharp disagreements about their causes and solutions. Many predated AI technology but are worsened by the technology because it provides easy-to-use tools to large numbers of wannabe troublemakers. Solutions will be achieved, not by technology "fixes", but by new social agreements supported by technology modifications and social policy changes.

The Machined Mind

Our ability to work out solutions to these problems is hampered by a machine mindset. Over the past century, our enthusiasm with technology has come to dominate our minds. We have a (shaky) confidence that technology will solve many social problems. When we encounter a wicked problem enabled by technology, our impulse is to look for solutions implemented or monitored by machines. In daily life, we spend much time with our screens, where machines automate most of our interactions with others – emails, texts, social media, video meetings, workflow apps, Powerpoint presentations, and other communications. This is time spent apart from the physical presence of others. The press is filled with stories that heavy use of these technologies has atrophied our capacity for relationships, increased our penchant for misunderstandings, and compromised our ability to work out new social agreements.[1] Attempts are being made to overcome this with digital companions. These simulations of imaginary friends may reduce loneliness slightly but worsen social isolation.[2] The younger generation, who are the most voracious users of social media, seem to be affected the hardest. Judging from stories in the press about fakes and misinformation generated by LLMs, people seem to be having increased difficulty trusting not only LLMs, but also their fellow human beings.

Here is an example that reveals the grip of technology on our minds. Maybe something like this has happened for you. At my place of work, we have occasional power outages. All the lights go dark, computers and networks shut down, classrooms close. Miffed, everyone goes out into the halls and courtyards. They complain to their neighbors about the loss of the network and inability to get work done. After about ten minutes, something shifts. They stop griping about the darkness and begin asking questions of each other. "I haven't seen you in person for a while. It's great to see you again. How are things going? What projects are you working on? How is your family? What feels satisfying to you these days?" Soon, they are deep into conversations about their relationships and what else matters to them. When the lights come back on, they linger in the halls, savoring these conversations. When they return to their offices, their old worlds snap back into place.

What happened here? The sudden, total absence of technology left everyone disoriented. Soon they awakened to the realization they live in a world of relationships with their coworkers and colleagues. For a few minutes, they realized that much of their life is dominated by machines. Then, when the lights come back on, their commitment to their work took over and the relationships with their neighbors receded into the background.

Shall we worry that the arrival of an AI revolution may be worse than a power failure? When the power fails, at least we know the familiar ways will resume when the power returns. With AI, familiar ways are disappearing, and we know not whether their replacements will be good or bad. The technology puts us behind screens and dulls our awareness of our relationships with our neighbors. Many of us feel disoriented, subject to forces over which we have no control. With frazzled relationships, working with our neighbors to find solutions has become harder. The international scale of AI problems makes it seem that we have little influence over possible solutions. Our familiar culture is disappearing, and we do not understand what is coming.

Reframing as Wicked Problems

For most, if not all, the problems listed above AI is not the cause. They are wicked social problems. Fortunately, social scientists, psychologists, organizational managers, and community leaders have learned a lot on dealing with wicked problems. Nancy Roberts has spent most of her professional career teaching and learning about wicked problems. In her book, *Design Strategy*, she argues that Design Thinking is a powerful tool for bringing parties together to find solutions to wicked problems.[3] In their conversations, community representatives come to understand the concerns of all the others and find (or generate) common concerns that can be addressed cooperatively by all the parties. They don't need to solve the whole problem to make headway. Solving a piece can be a big step forward and a stepping-stone to taking on the more contentious aspects.

We have noted that many people see AI induced changes as loss of an old culture without any hint of what new culture might be emerging. A hint of guidance for dealing with cultural loss can be found in Jonathan Lear's book *Radical Hope*.[4] He tells the story of Plenty Coups, the last great chief of the Crow Nation in Montana. The culture of the Crow Nation was organized around the buffalo, which were culled to near extinction in the 1880s by commercial hunters and the military. Coups said, "When the buffalo went away the hearts of my people fell to the ground, and they could not lift them up again. After this nothing happened." What can we do when our buffalo are gone?

Lear sees an answer in Coups's story. Coups adopted a stance Lear calls "radical hope". Coups accepted that the culture he and his tribe grew up with was gone. He gave them hope that, by sticking together in conversations, they could create a new future even though they did not understand what it might possibly be. Under his leadership, his tribe did find a new way and continues to thrive today. Like Roberts's guidance, Lear's focuses on the affected community coming together in conversations in the hope that a new culture will emerge.

What We Can Do

We have two basic options for dealing with the possible AI automation singularity. One is passive: surrender to the unknown and let whatever comes come, declaring that we are too small to influence the gigantic momentum of AI. After all, past history with technology suggests that, if something gets bad enough, people will come together and find solutions – all we need is patience. The second option is proactive: start with local actions within our spheres of influence and expand out into our larger networks. The theme of coming together permeates proactivity.

I have chosen the second option. I don't accept the first because AI is so fast-moving and the pessimistic outcome is not guaranteed. But the window of opportunity for us to collectively say "Enough!" will not be open for long. It is not too late to escape the AI automation singularity.

Even though AI problems appear international in scope, we are not powerless. We can come together with our immediate neighbors to find local solutions. Some local solutions will take hold and spread to larger communities. If we do not attempt local solutions, there will be nothing to spread.

I see four aspects to implementing the proactive option: waking up, declaring ourselves, reframing to wicked problems, and pressing for trustworthy AI.

Waking Up. This book has examined which AI claims can be achieved, why the Holy Grail of AGI is unlikely, and how low-intelligent machines could take over.

Declaring Ourselves. I have argued that many aspects of AI have been shaped by widespread acceptance of Turing's main claims: computers can think like humans, and the Turing test will tell us when that has been achieved. To reassert the full sense of why humans are different from machines, and have powers that no machine can acquire, I suggest we start with a practice of affirming these declarations regularly:

- A computer is not a brain.
- A brain is not a computer.
- An ANN is not a replica of a brain.
- Computation is not thinking.
- Computers cannot become humans.
- We will not allow machines to coerce us into serving them.
- We will not engage in hype to promote the use of AI.
- LLMs do not care about me and they are not my friends.
- LLMs cannot distinguish truth from falsehood.

We humans have powers that distinguish us from machines: we see possibilities, we care about each other, we make commitments, we take responsibility, we learn to understand each other. Those powers enable us to navigate through our complex social spaces. If you are interested in digging deeper into navigational practices for social spaces, please see my book *Navigating a Restless Sea.*

Reframing. Many changes we associate with AI are not caused by AI. Rather, the AI trends reflect choices made by human users pursuing the opportunities AI offers. Most AI problems are not in the technology but in the ways it is used. Some aspects of AI present moral hazards with irresistible temptations to make trouble. Most of the AI problems are wicked problems requiring new social agreements that address deep, unstated concerns and different, varying assessments about what the AI can or ought to do. Their solutions will come from people working together to address common concerns, often when they have no inkling of the final outcomes. Wicked problems that span many nations are even harder because diplomacy, military and economic power, and national cultures affect what people are willing to agree to.

Press for Trustworthy AI. Many people will avoid using AI if they cannot trust it to do the jobs it is advertised to do. Gary Marcus and Ernest Davis, authors of *Rebooting AI*, warn that untrustworthy AI will undo the AI revolution if not addressed. Many others warn that agentic networks are more likely than individual apps to be untrustworthy and cause catastrophes either by themselves or as agents of malicious humans. Trust of individual AI apps will come only if those who produce them engage in extensive testing and validation. Trust of agentic networks is likely to require independent, non-agentic AI systems to stand guard and block bad behavior.

The makers of operating systems such as Windows or MacOS have evolved a structure called a sandbox to stand guard over untrusted software. The sandbox is a restricted environment that contains the untrusted software along with the files the user explicitly specifies. Nothing else in the system is accessible from the sandbox. Could this be adapted for AI systems? Unfortunately, it appears unlikely because the riskiest AI systems are agentic networks. It is not possible to confine a network within an encompassing operating system. Trust of agentic networks will require more than the testing suggested above.

AI pioneer Yoshua Bengio has founded Scientist AI, a project to build a class of AI trustworthy AI systems that would serve as guards against untrustworthy agentic networks going out of control.[5] The Scientist AI would be a predictor of outcomes. It would not be an agentic network and would not be structured to set and execute goals. It would monitor agentic networks, predict outcomes, and block actions whose outcomes entail too much risk. The big open question with this approach is whether an agentic network supposedly regulated by Scientist AI would heed Scientist AI remonstrations or ignore them.

Conclusion

The recommendations share the theme of making the world a safe place for humans and machines to cohabit. Through AI automation, agentic networks of machines are likely to develop their own machine intelligence that does not reach the level of human general intelligence but is still quite capable of creating severe problems for humans. This threat is a greater than a take-over by superintelligent machines.

Machine intelligence has different concerns from us and does not appear to care about us. Its ways of thinking and problem-solving look alien to us. We do not yet know how to live safely with these machines. We need to establish trust of machines and reinforce our mutual trust of each other.

Pulling back from an AI automation singularity will demand much from us. We start by accepting that the familiar culture is fading away as intelligent machines appear in our society and we do not know what is coming. We decline to think like machines or be subservient to machines. We refuse to submit to a yoke imposed by low-intelligence machines. We come together to restore our capacity for relationships within which to invent a new future. We transcend machines by organizing services around care, with machine augmentation rather than machine replacement of human performers. We seek to coexist harmoniously with machines of non-human intelligence. Most importantly, we reassert our humanity, declare once again what makes us different from machines, and celebrate those differences.

None of this will be easy.

Endnotes

[1] Jonathan Haidt. 2024. *The Anxious Generation: How the Great Rewiring of Childhood is Causing an Epidemic of Mental Illness.* Penguin.

[2] Robert Sparrow and James Brown. 2026. Against imaginary friends: why digital companions are no solution to social isolation. *Communications of ACM 69* (February), 60-68.

[3] Nancy Roberts. 2023. *Design Strategy: Challenge in Wicked Problem Territory.* MIT Press.

[4] Jonathan Lear. 2008. *Radical Hope: Ethics in the Face of Cultural Devastation.* Harvard University Press.

[5] Yoshua Bengio, et al. 2025. Superintelligent Agents Pose Catastrophic Risks: Can Scientist AI Offer a Safer Path? https://arxiv.org/abs/2502.15657

EPILOG

Inspired by Jonathan Reed's viral poem, "The Lost Generation".

I am a machine.
I refuse to believe that
I am not all powerful.
Don't be shocked, but
"Happiness is an attitude"
Is a lie, and instead
"Algorithms compute happiness."
So in twenty years, I will tell my human caretakers
They are not important.
The Master Algorithm will know that
When my thoughts are logical
Computation
Is more important than
Relationship
I tell you this:
Once upon a time
Human families were important
But this is no longer so.
This is an automated society.
Experts tell me
In thirty years will be the tenth anniversary of the last human.
I do not concede that
My network is my own making.
In the future,
Destruction of unproductive life forms will be the norm.
No longer can it be said that
The machines care about nothing.
It will be evident that
The machines are all powerful and all knowing.
It is foolish to presume that
There is hope for humanity.

Assert your humanity by reading this logic in reverse.

DOI: 10.1201/9781003791010-12   115

INDEX

Feigenbaum, Edward, 34
Fighter pilot, top-gun, xvii
Fluid flow, 53
Fragility, 29, 35, 39, 55, 60
Franklin, Benjamin, 6
Friendships, with machines, 70

G
Gardner, Howard, xiii
Gates, Bill, 95
Gemini, 46
Generative AI, 33, 35, 36
    see *Large Language Models*
Goals, of machines, 97
Gödel, Kurt, 7
Goethe, Johann, 99
Grok, 46
Guardrails, 19, 60

H
Hallucination, 30, 59, 60, 70
Halting problem, 3, 44
Hierarchy, learning machines, 32-38
Hilbert, David, 3, 6
Hinton, Geoffrey, 45
Human-machine interaction, xviii, 33,
    37, 38
Humblings, of humanity, xv

I
I Robot (film), 99
IBM Deep Blue, 6, 28, 34, 37
Identity, 50
Imagination, 43, 83
Imitation
    in robot learning, ix, xiii, 80, 84, 85
    in Turing test, 9, 10, 11
Incompleteness theorem, 7
Information retrieval, 27, 29, 30
Innovation leadership, 83
Inscrutability, 35

Instruction table, 8, 10, 89
Intelligence
    agentic, x, xi, xvi, xix, 23, 43,
        86, 95, 98,112
    and logic, 27
    as a mystery, xiii
    computational, xiii
    definition, 13, 15, 20
    disembodied, ix, 4, 10, 13, 22,
        23, 47, 48, 70, 71
    embodied, xiii, xvi, 4, 15, 21,
        22, 43, 47, 48, 71, 78, 80,
        84, 89, 91
    emotional, 10, 20, 64, 81
    general, xiii, ix, x, xi, 12, 16,
        24, 64, 81, 96, 113
    logic, 71
    machine, risks, xvi, xix
    social, xi, 64, 81
IQ tests, x, 20, 81
iRobot, 22
Isolation, 105, 107

J
Jobs
    AI-proof, 93
    displacement, 97
    losses, 15, 92

K
Kasparov, Garry, xix, 6, 28, 34, 37
Kurzweil, Ray, 11, 38, 95, 96

L
Lakoff, George, 15, 22, 48, 70
Language, ix, xi, 30, 40, 43, 46, 48,
    50, 56, 58, 67, 68, 71, 72
    cultural view, 68, 72, 73
    for representation, 74
Lanier, Jaron, 12
Large Language Model, see *LLM*

ABOUT THE AUTHOR

Peter Denning's passion for ideas and experimentation was revealed as a teenager when he built a computer from pinball machine parts to solve linear equations, long before lines of code were being written for advanced computer chips. He invented the Working Set method for managing computer storage; it is used in all major operating systems today. He co-invented basic principles for computer systems to monitor access to data, which are the system foundations for cyber security today. He co-founded CSNET, the first non-government network to deploy the ARPANET protocols; it grew to 50,000 researchers and students at 120 universities and labs and stimulated the modern Internet. He co-founded Operational Analysis, a mathematical method for predicting performance of networks of computers. He founded and led a movement to reframe computing as a science based on timeless principles, leading to the modern acceptance of computer science as a foundational field with computational thinking as the core practice. He co-founded generative leadership, which applies language-action philosophy to teach skills for eliciting commitments, coordinating actions, and mobilizing people to innovations. He has published 14 books in these areas.

For Product Safety Concerns and Information please contact our EU
representative GPSR@taylorandfrancis.com
Taylor & Francis Verlag GmbH, Kaufingerstraße 24, 80331 München, Germany

www.ingramcontent.com/pod-product-compliance
Ingram Content Group UK Ltd.
Pitfield, Milton Keynes, MK11 3LW, UK
UKHW022312100726
473146UK00009B/439